C-2727

THIS IS YOUR **PASSBOOK**® FOR ...

# PERSONNEL COMPUTER SERVICES SPECIALIST

NATIONAL LEARNING CORPORATION®
passbooks.com

Copyright © 2020 by

**National Learning Corporation**

212 Michael Drive, Syosset, NY 11791
(516) 921-8888 • www.passbooks.com
E-mail: info@passbooks.com

PUBLISHED IN THE UNITED STATES OF AMERICA

# PASSBOOK® SERIES

THE *PASSBOOK® SERIES* has been created to prepare applicants and candidates for the ultimate academic battlefield – the examination room.

At some time in our lives, each and every one of us may be required to take an examination – for validation, matriculation, admission, qualification, registration, certification, or licensure.

Based on the assumption that every applicant or candidate has met the basic formal educational standards, has taken the required number of courses, and read the necessary texts, the *PASSBOOK® SERIES* furnishes the one special preparation which may assure passing with confidence, instead of failing with insecurity. Examination questions – together with answers – are furnished as the basic vehicle for study so that the mysteries of the examination and its compounding difficulties may be eliminated or diminished by a sure method.

This book is meant to help you pass your examination provided that you qualify and are serious in your objective.

The entire field is reviewed through the huge store of content information which is succinctly presented through a provocative and challenging approach – the question-and-answer method.

A climate of success is established by furnishing the correct answers at the end of each test.

You soon learn to recognize types of questions, forms of questions, and patterns of questioning. You may even begin to anticipate expected outcomes.

You perceive that many questions are repeated or adapted so that you can gain acute insights, which may enable you to score many sure points.

You learn how to confront new questions, or types of questions, and to attack them confidently and work out the correct answers.

You note objectives and emphases, and recognize pitfalls and dangers, so that you may make positive educational adjustments.

Moreover, you are kept fully informed in relation to new concepts, methods, practices, and directions in the field.

You discover that you arre actually taking the examination all the time: you are preparing for the examination by "taking" an examination, not by reading extraneous and/or supererogatory textbooks.

In short, this PASSBOOK®, used directedly, should be an important factor in helping you to pass your test.

# HOW TO TAKE A TEST

## I. YOU MUST PASS AN EXAMINATION

### A. *WHAT EVERY CANDIDATE SHOULD KNOW*

Examination applicants often ask us for help in preparing for the written test. What can I study in advance? What kinds of questions will be asked? How will the test be given? How will the papers be graded?

As an applicant for a civil service examination, you may be wondering about some of these things. Our purpose here is to suggest effective methods of advance study and to describe civil service examinations.

Your chances for success on this examination can be increased if you know how to prepare. Those "pre-examination jitters" can be reduced if you know what to expect. You can even experience an adventure in good citizenship if you know why civil service exams are given.

### B. *WHY ARE CIVIL SERVICE EXAMINATIONS GIVEN?*

Civil service examinations are important to you in two ways. As a citizen, you want public jobs filled by employees who know how to do their work. As a job seeker, you want a fair chance to compete for that job on an equal footing with other candidates. The best-known means of accomplishing this two-fold goal is the competitive examination.

Exams are widely publicized throughout the nation. They may be administered for jobs in federal, state, city, municipal, town or village governments or agencies.

Any citizen may apply, with some limitations, such as the age or residence of applicants. Your experience and education may be reviewed to see whether you meet the requirements for the particular examination. When these requirements exist, they are reasonable and applied consistently to all applicants. Thus, a competitive examination may cause you some uneasiness now, but it is your privilege and safeguard.

### C. *HOW ARE CIVIL SERVICE EXAMS DEVELOPED?*

Examinations are carefully written by trained technicians who are specialists in the field known as "psychological measurement," in consultation with recognized authorities in the field of work that the test will cover. These experts recommend the subject matter areas or skills to be tested; only those knowledges or skills important to your success on the job are included. The most reliable books and source materials available are used as references. Together, the experts and technicians judge the difficulty level of the questions.

Test technicians know how to phrase questions so that the problem is clearly stated. Their ethics do not permit "trick" or "catch" questions. Questions may have been tried out on sample groups, or subjected to statistical analysis, to determine their usefulness.

Written tests are often used in combination with performance tests, ratings of training and experience, and oral interviews. All of these measures combine to form the best-known means of finding the right person for the right job.

## II. HOW TO PASS THE WRITTEN TEST

### A. NATURE OF THE EXAMINATION

To prepare intelligently for civil service examinations, you should know how they differ from school examinations you have taken. In school you were assigned certain definite pages to read or subjects to cover. The examination questions were quite detailed and usually emphasized memory. Civil service exams, on the other hand, try to discover your present ability to perform the duties of a position, plus your potentiality to learn these duties. In other words, a civil service exam attempts to predict how successful you will be. Questions cover such a broad area that they cannot be as minute and detailed as school exam questions.

In the public service similar kinds of work, or positions, are grouped together in one "class." This process is known as *position-classification*. All the positions in a class are paid according to the salary range for that class. One class title covers all of these positions, and they are all tested by the same examination.

### B. FOUR BASIC STEPS

#### 1) Study the announcement

How, then, can you know what subjects to study? Our best answer is: "Learn as much as possible about the class of positions for which you've applied." The exam will test the knowledge, skills and abilities needed to do the work.

Your most valuable source of information about the position you want is the official exam announcement. This announcement lists the training and experience qualifications. Check these standards and apply only if you come reasonably close to meeting them.

The brief description of the position in the examination announcement offers some clues to the subjects which will be tested. Think about the job itself. Review the duties in your mind. Can you perform them, or are there some in which you are rusty? Fill in the blank spots in your preparation.

Many jurisdictions preview the written test in the exam announcement by including a section called "Knowledge and Abilities Required," "Scope of the Examination," or some similar heading. Here you will find out specifically what fields will be tested.

#### 2) Review your own background

Once you learn in general what the position is all about, and what you need to know to do the work, ask yourself which subjects you already know fairly well and which need improvement. You may wonder whether to concentrate on improving your strong areas or on building some background in your fields of weakness. When the announcement has specified "some knowledge" or "considerable knowledge," or has used adjectives like "beginning principles of…" or "advanced … methods," you can get a clue as to the number and difficulty of questions to be asked in any given field. More questions, and hence broader coverage, would be included for those subjects which are more important in the work. Now weigh your strengths and weaknesses against the job requirements and prepare accordingly.

### 3) Determine the level of the position

Another way to tell how intensively you should prepare is to understand the level of the job for which you are applying. Is it the entering level? In other words, is this the position in which beginners in a field of work are hired? Or is it an intermediate or advanced level? Sometimes this is indicated by such words as "Junior" or "Senior" in the class title. Other jurisdictions use Roman numerals to designate the level – Clerk I, Clerk II, for example. The word "Supervisor" sometimes appears in the title. If the level is not indicated by the title, check the description of duties. Will you be working under very close supervision, or will you have responsibility for independent decisions in this work?

### 4) Choose appropriate study materials

Now that you know the subjects to be examined and the relative amount of each subject to be covered, you can choose suitable study materials. For beginning level jobs, or even advanced ones, if you have a pronounced weakness in some aspect of your training, read a modern, standard textbook in that field. Be sure it is up to date and has general coverage. Such books are normally available at your library, and the librarian will be glad to help you locate one. For entry-level positions, questions of appropriate difficulty are chosen – neither highly advanced questions, nor those too simple. Such questions require careful thought but not advanced training.

If the position for which you are applying is technical or advanced, you will read more advanced, specialized material. If you are already familiar with the basic principles of your field, elementary textbooks would waste your time. Concentrate on advanced textbooks and technical periodicals. Think through the concepts and review difficult problems in your field.

These are all general sources. You can get more ideas on your own initiative, following these leads. For example, training manuals and publications of the government agency which employs workers in your field can be useful, particularly for technical and professional positions. A letter or visit to the government department involved may result in more specific study suggestions, and certainly will provide you with a more definite idea of the exact nature of the position you are seeking.

## III. KINDS OF TESTS

Tests are used for purposes other than measuring knowledge and ability to perform specified duties. For some positions, it is equally important to test ability to make adjustments to new situations or to profit from training. In others, basic mental abilities not dependent on information are essential. Questions which test these things may not appear as pertinent to the duties of the position as those which test for knowledge and information. Yet they are often highly important parts of a fair examination. For very general questions, it is almost impossible to help you direct your study efforts. What we can do is to point out some of the more common of these general abilities needed in public service positions and describe some typical questions.

### 1) General information

Broad, general information has been found useful for predicting job success in some kinds of work. This is tested in a variety of ways, from vocabulary lists to questions about current events. Basic background in some field of work, such as sociology or economics, may be sampled in a group of questions. Often these are principles which have become familiar to most persons through exposure rather than through formal training. It is difficult to advise you how to study for these questions; being alert to the world around you is our best suggestion.

2) Verbal ability

An example of an ability needed in many positions is verbal or language ability. Verbal ability is, in brief, the ability to use and understand words. Vocabulary and grammar tests are typical measures of this ability. Reading comprehension or paragraph interpretation questions are common in many kinds of civil service tests. You are given a paragraph of written material and asked to find its central meaning.

3) Numerical ability

Number skills can be tested by the familiar arithmetic problem, by checking paired lists of numbers to see which are alike and which are different, or by interpreting charts and graphs. In the latter test, a graph may be printed in the test booklet which you are asked to use as the basis for answering questions.

4) Observation

A popular test for law-enforcement positions is the observation test. A picture is shown to you for several minutes, then taken away. Questions about the picture test your ability to observe both details and larger elements.

5) Following directions

In many positions in the public service, the employee must be able to carry out written instructions dependably and accurately. You may be given a chart with several columns, each column listing a variety of information. The questions require you to carry out directions involving the information given in the chart.

6) Skills and aptitudes

Performance tests effectively measure some manual skills and aptitudes. When the skill is one in which you are trained, such as typing or shorthand, you can practice. These tests are often very much like those given in business school or high school courses. For many of the other skills and aptitudes, however, no short-time preparation can be made. Skills and abilities natural to you or that you have developed throughout your lifetime are being tested.

Many of the general questions just described provide all the data needed to answer the questions and ask you to use your reasoning ability to find the answers. Your best preparation for these tests, as well as for tests of facts and ideas, is to be at your physical and mental best. You, no doubt, have your own methods of getting into an exam-taking mood and keeping "in shape." The next section lists some ideas on this subject.

IV.  KINDS OF QUESTIONS

Only rarely is the "essay" question, which you answer in narrative form, used in civil service tests. Civil service tests are usually of the short-answer type. Full instructions for answering these questions will be given to you at the examination. But in case this is your first experience with short-answer questions and separate answer sheets, here is what you need to know:

## 1) Multiple-choice Questions

Most popular of the short-answer questions is the "multiple choice" or "best answer" question. It can be used, for example, to test for factual knowledge, ability to solve problems or judgment in meeting situations found at work.

A multiple-choice question is normally one of three types—

- It can begin with an incomplete statement followed by several possible endings. You are to find the one ending which *best* completes the statement, although some of the others may not be entirely wrong.
- It can also be a complete statement in the form of a question which is answered by choosing one of the statements listed.
- It can be in the form of a problem – again you select the best answer.

Here is an example of a multiple-choice question with a discussion which should give you some clues as to the method for choosing the right answer:

When an employee has a complaint about his assignment, the action which will *best* help him overcome his difficulty is to
  A. discuss his difficulty with his coworkers
  B. take the problem to the head of the organization
  C. take the problem to the person who gave him the assignment
  D. say nothing to anyone about his complaint

In answering this question, you should study each of the choices to find which is best. Consider choice "A" – Certainly an employee may discuss his complaint with fellow employees, but no change or improvement can result, and the complaint remains unresolved. Choice "B" is a poor choice since the head of the organization probably does not know what assignment you have been given, and taking your problem to him is known as "going over the head" of the supervisor. The supervisor, or person who made the assignment, is the person who can clarify it or correct any injustice. Choice "C" is, therefore, correct. To say nothing, as in choice "D," is unwise. Supervisors have and interest in knowing the problems employees are facing, and the employee is seeking a solution to his problem.

## 2) True/False Questions

The "true/false" or "right/wrong" form of question is sometimes used. Here a complete statement is given. Your job is to decide whether the statement is right or wrong.

SAMPLE: A roaming cell-phone call to a nearby city costs less than a non-roaming call to a distant city.

This statement is wrong, or false, since roaming calls are more expensive.
This is not a complete list of all possible question forms, although most of the others are variations of these common types. You will always get complete directions for

answering questions.  Be sure you understand *how* to mark your answers – ask questions until you do.


## V.  RECORDING YOUR ANSWERS

Computer terminals are used more and more today for many different kinds of exams.

For an examination with very few applicants, you may be told to record your answers in the test booklet itself.  Separate answer sheets are much more common.  If this separate answer sheet is to be scored by machine – and this is often the case – it is highly important that you mark your answers correctly in order to get credit.

An electronic scoring machine is often used in civil service offices because of the speed with which papers can be scored.  Machine-scored answer sheets must be marked with a pencil, which will be given to you.  This pencil has a high graphite content which responds to the electronic scoring machine.  As a matter of fact, stray dots may register as answers, so do not let your pencil rest on the answer sheet while you are pondering the correct answer.  Also, if your pencil lead breaks or is otherwise defective, ask for another.

Since the answer sheet will be dropped in a slot in the scoring machine, be careful not to bend the corners or get the paper crumpled.

The answer sheet normally has five vertical columns of numbers, with 30 numbers to a column.  These numbers correspond to the question numbers in your test booklet.  After each number, going across the page are four or five pairs of dotted lines.  These short dotted lines have small letters or numbers above them.  The first two pairs may also have a "T" or "F" above the letters.  This indicates that the first two pairs only are to be used if the questions are of the true-false type.  If the questions are multiple choice, disregard the "T" and "F" and pay attention only to the small letters or numbers.

Answer your questions in the manner of the sample that follows:

32.  The largest city in the United States is
   A.  Washington, D.C.
   B.  New York City
   C.  Chicago
   D.  Detroit
   E.  San Francisco

1) Choose the answer you think is best.  (New York City is the largest, so "B" is correct.)
2) Find the row of dotted lines numbered the same as the question you are answering.  (Find row number 32)
3) Find the pair of dotted lines corresponding to the answer.  (Find the pair of lines under the mark "B.")
4) Make a solid black mark between the dotted lines.


## VI. BEFORE THE TEST

Common sense will help you find procedures to follow to get ready for an examination.  Too many of us, however, overlook these sensible measures.  Indeed, nervousness and fatigue have been found to be the most serious reasons why applicants fail to do their best on civil service tests. Here is a list of reminders:

- Begin your preparation early – Don't wait until the last minute to go scurrying around for books and materials or to find out what the position is all about.
- Prepare continuously – An hour a night for a week is better than an all-night cram session. This has been definitely established. What is more, a night a week for a month will return better dividends than crowding your study into a shorter period of time.
- Locate the place of the exam – You have been sent a notice telling you when and where to report for the examination. If the location is in a different town or otherwise unfamiliar to you, it would be well to inquire the best route and learn something about the building.
- Relax the night before the test – Allow your mind to rest. Do not study at all that night. Plan some mild recreation or diversion; then go to bed early and get a good night's sleep.
- Get up early enough to make a leisurely trip to the place for the test – This way unforeseen events, traffic snarls, unfamiliar buildings, etc. will not upset you.
- Dress comfortably – A written test is not a fashion show. You will be known by number and not by name, so wear something comfortable.
- Leave excess paraphernalia at home – Shopping bags and odd bundles will get in your way. You need bring only the items mentioned in the official notice you received; usually everything you need is provided. Do not bring reference books to the exam. They will only confuse those last minutes and be taken away from you when in the test room.
- Arrive somewhat ahead of time – If because of transportation schedules you must get there very early, bring a newspaper or magazine to take your mind off yourself while waiting.
- Locate the examination room – When you have found the proper room, you will be directed to the seat or part of the room where you will sit. Sometimes you are given a sheet of instructions to read while you are waiting. Do not fill out any forms until you are told to do so; just read them and be prepared.
- Relax and prepare to listen to the instructions
- If you have any physical problem that may keep you from doing your best, be sure to tell the test administrator. If you are sick or in poor health, you really cannot do your best on the exam. You can come back and take the test some other time.

## VII. AT THE TEST

The day of the test is here and you have the test booklet in your hand. The temptation to get going is very strong. Caution! There is more to success than knowing the right answers. You must know how to identify your papers and understand variations in the type of short-answer question used in this particular examination. Follow these suggestions for maximum results from your efforts:

### 1) Cooperate with the monitor

The test administrator has a duty to create a situation in which you can be as much at ease as possible. He will give instructions, tell you when to begin, check to see that you are marking your answer sheet correctly, and so on. He is not there to guard you, although he will see that your competitors do not take unfair advantage. He wants to help you do your best.

### 2) Listen to all instructions

Don't jump the gun! Wait until you understand all directions. In most civil service tests you get more time than you need to answer the questions. So don't be in a hurry. Read each word of instructions until you clearly understand the meaning. Study the examples, listen to all announcements and follow directions. Ask questions if you do not understand what to do.

### 3) Identify your papers

Civil service exams are usually identified by number only. You will be assigned a number; you must not put your name on your test papers. Be sure to copy your number correctly. Since more than one exam may be given, copy your exact examination title.

### 4) Plan your time

Unless you are told that a test is a "speed" or "rate of work" test, speed itself is usually not important. Time enough to answer all the questions will be provided, but this does not mean that you have all day. An overall time limit has been set. Divide the total time (in minutes) by the number of questions to determine the approximate time you have for each question.

### 5) Do not linger over difficult questions

If you come across a difficult question, mark it with a paper clip (useful to have along) and come back to it when you have been through the booklet. One caution if you do this – be sure to skip a number on your answer sheet as well. Check often to be sure that you have not lost your place and that you are marking in the row numbered the same as the question you are answering.

### 6) Read the questions

Be sure you know what the question asks! Many capable people are unsuccessful because they failed to *read* the questions correctly.

### 7) Answer all questions

Unless you have been instructed that a penalty will be deducted for incorrect answers, it is better to guess than to omit a question.

### 8) Speed tests

It is often better NOT to guess on speed tests. It has been found that on timed tests people are tempted to spend the last few seconds before time is called in marking answers at random – without even reading them – in the hope of picking up a few extra points. To discourage this practice, the instructions may warn you that your score will be "corrected" for guessing. That is, a penalty will be applied. The incorrect answers will be deducted from the correct ones, or some other penalty formula will be used.

## 9) Review your answers

If you finish before time is called, go back to the questions you guessed or omitted to give them further thought. Review other answers if you have time.

## 10) Return your test materials

If you are ready to leave before others have finished or time is called, take ALL your materials to the monitor and leave quietly. Never take any test material with you. The monitor can discover whose papers are not complete, and taking a test booklet may be grounds for disqualification.

## VIII. EXAMINATION TECHNIQUES

1) Read the general instructions carefully. These are usually printed on the first page of the exam booklet. As a rule, these instructions refer to the timing of the examination; the fact that you should not start work until the signal and must stop work at a signal, etc. If there are any *special* instructions, such as a choice of questions to be answered, make sure that you note this instruction carefully.

2) When you are ready to start work on the examination, that is as soon as the signal has been given, read the instructions to each question booklet, underline any key words or phrases, such as *least, best, outline, describe* and the like. In this way you will tend to answer as requested rather than discover on reviewing your paper that you *listed without describing*, that you selected the *worst* choice rather than the *best* choice, etc.

3) If the examination is of the objective or multiple-choice type – that is, each question will also give a series of possible answers: A, B, C or D, and you are called upon to select the best answer and write the letter next to that answer on your answer paper – it is advisable to start answering each question in turn. There may be anywhere from 50 to 100 such questions in the three or four hours allotted and you can see how much time would be taken if you read through all the questions before beginning to answer any. Furthermore, if you come across a question or group of questions which you know would be difficult to answer, it would undoubtedly affect your handling of all the other questions.

4) If the examination is of the essay type and contains but a few questions, it is a moot point as to whether you should read all the questions before starting to answer any one. Of course, if you are given a choice – say five out of seven and the like – then it is essential to read all the questions so you can eliminate the two that are most difficult. If, however, you are asked to answer all the questions, there may be danger in trying to answer the easiest one first because you may find that you will spend too much time on it. The best technique is to answer the first question, then proceed to the second, etc.

5) Time your answers. Before the exam begins, write down the time it started, then add the time allowed for the examination and write down the time it must be completed, then divide the time available somewhat as follows:

- If 3-1/2 hours are allowed, that would be 210 minutes. If you have 80 objective-type questions, that would be an average of 2-1/2 minutes per question. Allow yourself no more than 2 minutes per question, or a total of 160 minutes, which will permit about 50 minutes to review.
- If for the time allotment of 210 minutes there are 7 essay questions to answer, that would average about 30 minutes a question. Give yourself only 25 minutes per question so that you have about 35 minutes to review.

6) The most important instruction is to *read each question* and make sure you know what is wanted. The second most important instruction is to *time yourself properly* so that you answer every question. The third most important instruction is to *answer every question*. Guess if you have to but include something for each question. Remember that you will receive no credit for a blank and will probably receive some credit if you write something in answer to an essay question. If you guess a letter – say "B" for a multiple-choice question – you may have guessed right. If you leave a blank as an answer to a multiple-choice question, the examiners may respect your feelings but it will not add a point to your score. Some exams may penalize you for wrong answers, so in such cases *only*, you may not want to guess unless you have some basis for your answer.

7) Suggestions
   a. Objective-type questions
      1. Examine the question booklet for proper sequence of pages and questions
      2. Read all instructions carefully
      3. Skip any question which seems too difficult; return to it after all other questions have been answered
      4. Apportion your time properly; do not spend too much time on any single question or group of questions
      5. Note and underline key words – *all, most, fewest, least, best, worst, same, opposite,* etc.
      6. Pay particular attention to negatives
      7. Note unusual option, e.g., unduly long, short, complex, different or similar in content to the body of the question
      8. Observe the use of "hedging" words – *probably, may, most likely,* etc.
      9. Make sure that your answer is put next to the same number as the question
      10. Do not second-guess unless you have good reason to believe the second answer is definitely more correct
      11. Cross out original answer if you decide another answer is more accurate; do not erase until you are ready to hand your paper in
      12. Answer all questions; guess unless instructed otherwise
      13. Leave time for review

   b. Essay questions
      1. Read each question carefully
      2. Determine exactly what is wanted. Underline key words or phrases.
      3. Decide on outline or paragraph answer

4. Include many different points and elements unless asked to develop any one or two points or elements
5. Show impartiality by giving pros and cons unless directed to select one side only
6. Make and write down any assumptions you find necessary to answer the questions
7. Watch your English, grammar, punctuation and choice of words
8. Time your answers; don't crowd material

8) Answering the essay question

Most essay questions can be answered by framing the specific response around several key words or ideas.  Here are a few such key words or ideas:

M's:  manpower, materials, methods, money, management
P's:  purpose, program, policy, plan, procedure, practice, problems, pitfalls, personnel, public relations
  a. Six basic steps in handling problems:
    1. Preliminary plan and background development
    2. Collect information, data and facts
    3. Analyze and interpret information, data and facts
    4. Analyze and develop solutions as well as make recommendations
    5. Prepare report and sell recommendations
    6. Install recommendations and follow up effectiveness

  b. Pitfalls to avoid
    1. *Taking things for granted* – A statement of the situation does not necessarily imply that each of the elements is necessarily true; for example, a complaint may be invalid and biased so that all that can be taken for granted is that a complaint has been registered
    2. *Considering only one side of a situation* – Wherever possible, indicate several alternatives and then point out the reasons you selected the best one
    3. *Failing to indicate follow up* – Whenever your answer indicates action on your part, make certain that you will take proper follow-up action to see how successful your recommendations, procedures or actions turn out to be
    4. *Taking too long in answering any single question* – Remember to time your answers properly

## IX.  AFTER THE TEST

Scoring procedures differ in detail among civil service jurisdictions although the general principles are the same.  Whether the papers are hand-scored or graded by machine we have described, they are nearly always graded by number.  That is, the person who marks the paper knows only the number – never the name – of the applicant.  Not until all the papers have been graded will they be matched with names.  If other tests, such as training and experience or oral interview ratings have been given, scores will be combined. Different parts of the examination usually have different weights. For example, the written test might count 60 percent of the final grade, and a rating of training and experience 40 percent. In many jurisdictions, veterans will have a certain number of points added to their grades.

After the final grade has been determined, the names are placed in grade order and an eligible list is established. There are various methods for resolving ties between those who get the same final grade – probably the most common is to place first the name of the person whose application was received first. Job offers are made from the eligible list in the order the names appear on it. You will be notified of your grade and your rank as soon as all these computations have been made. This will be done as rapidly as possible.

People who are found to meet the requirements in the announcement are called "eligibles." Their names are put on a list of eligible candidates. An eligible's chances of getting a job depend on how high he stands on this list and how fast agencies are filling jobs from the list.

When a job is to be filled from a list of eligibles, the agency asks for the names of people on the list of eligibles for that job. When the civil service commission receives this request, it sends to the agency the names of the three people highest on this list. Or, if the job to be filled has specialized requirements, the office sends the agency the names of the top three persons who meet these requirements from the general list.

The appointing officer makes a choice from among the three people whose names were sent to him. If the selected person accepts the appointment, the names of the others are put back on the list to be considered for future openings.

That is the rule in hiring from all kinds of eligible lists, whether they are for typist, carpenter, chemist, or something else. For every vacancy, the appointing officer has his choice of any one of the top three eligibles on the list. This explains why the person whose name is on top of the list sometimes does not get an appointment when some of the persons lower on the list do. If the appointing officer chooses the second or third eligible, the No. 1 eligible does not get a job at once, but stays on the list until he is appointed or the list is terminated.

## X. HOW TO PASS THE INTERVIEW TEST

The examination for which you applied requires an oral interview test. You have already taken the written test and you are now being called for the interview test – the final part of the formal examination.

You may think that it is not possible to prepare for an interview test and that there are no procedures to follow during an interview. Our purpose is to point out some things you can do in advance that will help you and some good rules to follow and pitfalls to avoid while you are being interviewed.

*What is an interview supposed to test?*

The written examination is designed to test the technical knowledge and competence of the candidate; the oral is designed to evaluate intangible qualities, not readily measured otherwise, and to establish a list showing the relative fitness of each candidate – as measured against his competitors – for the position sought. Scoring is not on the basis of "right" and "wrong," but on a sliding scale of values ranging from "not passable" to "outstanding." As a matter of fact, it is possible to achieve a relatively low score without a single "incorrect" answer because of evident weakness in the qualities being measured.

Occasionally, an examination may consist entirely of an oral test – either an individual or a group oral. In such cases, information is sought concerning the technical knowledges and abilities of the candidate, since there has been no written examination for this purpose. More commonly, however, an oral test is used to supplement a written examination.

*Who conducts interviews?*

The composition of oral boards varies among different jurisdictions. In nearly all, a representative of the personnel department serves as chairman. One of the members of the board may be a representative of the department in which the candidate would work. In some cases, "outside experts" are used, and, frequently, a businessman or some other representative of the general public is asked to serve. Labor and management or other special groups may be represented. The aim is to secure the services of experts in the appropriate field.

However the board is composed, it is a good idea (and not at all improper or unethical) to ascertain in advance of the interview who the members are and what groups they represent. When you are introduced to them, you will have some idea of their backgrounds and interests, and at least you will not stutter and stammer over their names.

*What should be done before the interview?*

While knowledge about the board members is useful and takes some of the surprise element out of the interview, there is other preparation which is more substantive. It *is* possible to prepare for an oral interview – in several ways:

**1) Keep a copy of your application and review it carefully before the interview**

This may be the only document before the oral board, and the starting point of the interview. Know what education and experience you have listed there, and the sequence and dates of all of it. Sometimes the board will ask you to review the highlights of your experience for them; you should not have to hem and haw doing it.

**2) Study the class specification and the examination announcement**

Usually, the oral board has one or both of these to guide them. The qualities, characteristics or knowledges required by the position sought are stated in these documents. They offer valuable clues as to the nature of the oral interview. For example, if the job involves supervisory responsibilities, the announcement will usually indicate that knowledge of modern supervisory methods and the qualifications of the candidate as a supervisor will be tested. If so, you can expect such questions, frequently in the form of a hypothetical situation which you are expected to solve. NEVER go into an oral without knowledge of the duties and responsibilities of the job you seek.

**3) Think through each qualification required**

Try to visualize the kind of questions you would ask if you were a board member. How well could you answer them? Try especially to appraise your own knowledge and background in each area, *measured against the job sought*, and identify any areas in which you are weak. Be critical and realistic – do not flatter yourself.

**4) Do some general reading in areas in which you feel you may be weak**

For example, if the job involves supervision and your past experience has NOT, some general reading in supervisory methods and practices, particularly in the field of human relations, might be useful. Do NOT study agency procedures or detailed manuals. The oral board will be testing your understanding and capacity, not your memory.

**5) Get a good night's sleep and watch your general health and mental attitude**

You will want a clear head at the interview. Take care of a cold or any other minor ailment, and of course, no hangovers.

*What should be done on the day of the interview?*

Now comes the day of the interview itself. Give yourself plenty of time to get there. Plan to arrive somewhat ahead of the scheduled time, particularly if your appointment is in the fore part of the day. If a previous candidate fails to appear, the board might be ready for you a bit early. By early afternoon an oral board is almost invariably behind schedule if there are many candidates, and you may have to wait. Take along a book or magazine to read, or your application to review, but leave any extraneous material in the waiting room when you go in for your interview. In any event, relax and compose yourself.

The matter of dress is important. The board is forming impressions about you – from your experience, your manners, your attitude, and your appearance. Give your personal appearance careful attention. Dress your best, but not your flashiest. Choose conservative, appropriate clothing, and be sure it is immaculate. This is a business interview, and your appearance should indicate that you regard it as such. Besides, being well groomed and properly dressed will help boost your confidence.

Sooner or later, someone will call your name and escort you into the interview room. *This is it.* From here on you are on your own. It is too late for any more preparation. But remember, you asked for this opportunity to prove your fitness, and you are here because your request was granted.

*What happens when you go in?*

The usual sequence of events will be as follows: The clerk (who is often the board stenographer) will introduce you to the chairman of the oral board, who will introduce you to the other members of the board. Acknowledge the introductions before you sit down. Do not be surprised if you find a microphone facing you or a stenotypist sitting by. Oral interviews are usually recorded in the event of an appeal or other review.

Usually the chairman of the board will open the interview by reviewing the highlights of your education and work experience from your application – primarily for the benefit of the other members of the board, as well as to get the material into the record. Do not interrupt or comment unless there is an error or significant misinterpretation; if that is the case, do not hesitate. But do not quibble about insignificant matters. Also, he will usually ask you some question about your education, experience or your present job – partly to get you to start talking and to establish the interviewing "rapport." He may start the actual questioning, or turn it over to one of the other members. Frequently, each member undertakes the questioning on a particular area, one in which he is perhaps most competent, so you can expect each member to participate in the examination. Because time is limited, you may also expect some rather abrupt switches in the direction the questioning takes, so do not be upset by it. Normally, a board member will not pursue a single line of questioning unless he discovers a particular strength or weakness.

After each member has participated, the chairman will usually ask whether any member has any further questions, then will ask you if you have anything you wish to add. Unless you are expecting this question, it may floor you. Worse, it may start you off on an extended, extemporaneous speech. The board is not usually seeking more information. The question is principally to offer you a last opportunity to present further qualifications or to indicate that you have nothing to add. So, if you feel that a significant qualification or characteristic has been overlooked, it is proper to point it out in a sentence or so. Do not compliment the board on the thoroughness of their examination – they have been sketchy, and you know it. If you wish, merely say, "No thank you, I have nothing further to add." This is a point where you can "talk yourself out" of a good impression or fail to present an important bit of information. Remember, *you close the interview yourself.*

The chairman will then say, "That is all, Mr. _____, thank you." Do not be startled; the interview is over, and quicker than you think. Thank him, gather your belongings and take your leave. Save your sigh of relief for the other side of the door.

*How to put your best foot forward*

Throughout this entire process, you may feel that the board individually and collectively is trying to pierce your defenses, seek out your hidden weaknesses and embarrass and confuse you. Actually, this is not true. They are obliged to make an appraisal of your qualifications for the job you are seeking, and they want to see you in your best light. Remember, they must interview all candidates and a non-cooperative candidate may become a failure in spite of their best efforts to bring out his qualifications. Here are 15 suggestions that will help you:

**1) Be natural – Keep your attitude confident, not cocky**

If you are not confident that you can do the job, do not expect the board to be. Do not apologize for your weaknesses, try to bring out your strong points. The board is interested in a positive, not negative, presentation. Cockiness will antagonize any board member and make him wonder if you are covering up a weakness by a false show of strength.

**2) Get comfortable, but don't lounge or sprawl**

Sit erectly but not stiffly. A careless posture may lead the board to conclude that you are careless in other things, or at least that you are not impressed by the importance of the occasion. Either conclusion is natural, even if incorrect. Do not fuss with your clothing, a pencil or an ashtray. Your hands may occasionally be useful to emphasize a point; do not let them become a point of distraction.

**3) Do not wisecrack or make small talk**

This is a serious situation, and your attitude should show that you consider it as such. Further, the time of the board is limited – they do not want to waste it, and neither should you.

**4) Do not exaggerate your experience or abilities**

In the first place, from information in the application or other interviews and sources, the board may know more about you than you think. Secondly, you probably will not get away with it. An experienced board is rather adept at spotting such a situation, so do not take the chance.

**5) If you know a board member, do not make a point of it, yet do not hide it**

Certainly you are not fooling him, and probably not the other members of the board. Do not try to take advantage of your acquaintanceship – it will probably do you little good.

**6) Do not dominate the interview**

Let the board do that. They will give you the clues – do not assume that you have to do all the talking. Realize that the board has a number of questions to ask you, and do not try to take up all the interview time by showing off your extensive knowledge of the answer to the first one.

**7) Be attentive**

You only have 20 minutes or so, and you should keep your attention at its sharpest throughout. When a member is addressing a problem or question to you, give him your undivided attention. Address your reply principally to him, but do not exclude the other board members.

**8) Do not interrupt**

A board member may be stating a problem for you to analyze. He will ask you a question when the time comes. Let him state the problem, and wait for the question.

**9) Make sure you understand the question**

Do not try to answer until you are sure what the question is. If it is not clear, restate it in your own words or ask the board member to clarify it for you. However, do not haggle about minor elements.

**10) Reply promptly but not hastily**

A common entry on oral board rating sheets is "candidate responded readily," or "candidate hesitated in replies." Respond as promptly and quickly as you can, but do not jump to a hasty, ill-considered answer.

**11) Do not be peremptory in your answers**

A brief answer is proper – but do not fire your answer back. That is a losing game from your point of view. The board member can probably ask questions much faster than you can answer them.

**12) Do not try to create the answer you think the board member wants**

He is interested in what kind of mind you have and how it works – not in playing games. Furthermore, he can usually spot this practice and will actually grade you down on it.

**13) Do not switch sides in your reply merely to agree with a board member**

Frequently, a member will take a contrary position merely to draw you out and to see if you are willing and able to defend your point of view. Do not start a debate, yet do not surrender a good position. If a position is worth taking, it is worth defending.

## 14) Do not be afraid to admit an error in judgment if you are shown to be wrong

The board knows that you are forced to reply without any opportunity for careful consideration. Your answer may be demonstrably wrong. If so, admit it and get on with the interview.

## 15) Do not dwell at length on your present job

The opening question may relate to your present assignment. Answer the question but do not go into an extended discussion. You are being examined for a *new* job, not your present one. As a matter of fact, try to phrase ALL your answers in terms of the job for which you are being examined.

*Basis of Rating*

Probably you will forget most of these "do's" and "don'ts" when you walk into the oral interview room. Even remembering them all will not ensure you a passing grade. Perhaps you did not have the qualifications in the first place. But remembering them will help you to put your best foot forward, without treading on the toes of the board members.

Rumor and popular opinion to the contrary notwithstanding, an oral board wants you to make the best appearance possible. They know you are under pressure – but they also want to see how you respond to it as a guide to what your reaction would be under the pressures of the job you seek. They will be influenced by the degree of poise you display, the personal traits you show and the manner in which you respond.

ABOUT THIS BOOK

This book contains tests divided into Examination Sections. Go through each test, answering every question in the margin. At the end of each test look at the answer key and check your answers. On the ones you got wrong, look at the right answer choice and learn. Do not fill in the answers first. Do not memorize the questions and answers, but understand the answer and principles involved. On your test, the questions will likely be different from the samples. Questions are changed and new ones added. If you understand these past questions you should have success with any changes that arise. Tests may consist of several types of questions. We have additional books on each subject should more study be advisable or necessary for you. Finally, the more you study, the better prepared you will be. This book is intended to be the last thing you study before you walk into the examination room. Prior study of relevant texts is also recommended. NLC publishes some of these in our Fundamental Series. Knowledge and good sense are important factors in passing your exam. Good luck also helps. So now study this Passbook, absorb the material contained within and take that knowledge into the examination. Then do your best to pass that exam.

———

# EXAMINATION SECTION

# EXAMINATION SECTION
## TEST 1

DIRECTIONS:   Each question or incomplete statement is followed by several suggested answers or completions. Select the one that BEST answers the question or completes the statement. *PRINT THE LETTER OF THE CORRECT ANSWER IN THE SPACE AT THE RIGHT.*

1. The speed disparity between adjacent devices can cause problems with an interface. These problems are usually resolved by temporarily storing input in a(n)      1.____

   A.   channel
   C.   register
   B.   control unit
   D.   buffer

2. A typical computer spends most of its time      2.____

   A.   compiling
   B.   waiting for input or output
   C.   executing instructions
   D.   interpreting commands

3. What is the basic input device on a small computer?      3.____

   A.   Keyboard      B.   Cursor      C.   Mouse      D.   Processor

4. When two hardware devices want to communicate, they will FIRST exchange _____ signals.      4.____

   A.   interrupt      B.   protocol      C.   interface      D.   boot

5. Which of the following is retrieved and executed by the processor?      5.____

   A.   Instructions
   C.   Information
   B.   Clock pulses
   D.   Data

6. What type of architecture is used by most microcomputers?      6.____

   A.   Standard
   C.   Single-bus
   B.   Serial
   D.   Multiple-bus

7. Typically, _____ is NOT a problem associated with a computer's main memory.      7.____

   A.   cost
   C.   capacity
   B.   volatility
   D.   speed

8. Which of the following types of memory management is the SIMPLEST?      8.____

   A.   Sector-oriented
   C.   Block-oriented
   B.   Dynamic
   D.   Fixed partition

9. What is the term for the time during which a disk drive is brought up to operating speed and the access device is positioned?      9.____

   A.   E-time
   C.   Seek time
   B.   Rotational delay
   D.   Access time

10.  What type of code is written by programmers?                                    10.____

   A.  Load module                        B.  Source
   C.  Object                             D.  Operating

11.  A _____ is the basic output device on a small computer.                      11.____

   A.  printer                            B.  keyboard
   C.  display screen                     D.  hard disk

12.  Which of the following serves to manage a computer's resources?                12.____

   A.  User                               B.  Operating system
   C.  Programmer                         D.  Software

13.  A computer processes data into                                                 13.____

   A.  information                        B.  pulses
   C.  code                               D.  facts

14.  What is the term for the entity used to link external devices to a small computer system?   14.____

   A.  Interface                          B.  Network
   C.  Plug-in                            D.  Modem

15.  For a transaction processing application, a _____ file organization should be selected.   15.____

   A.  sequential                         B.  indexed
   C.  direct                             D.  random

16.  Which element of a microcomputer directly controls input and output?           16.____

   A.  Buffer                             B.  Processor
   C.  Bus                                D.  Control unit

17.  A computer's data and program instructions are stored in                       17.____

   A.  memory                             B.  the video buffer
   C.  a program                          D.  an output port

18.  What is the term for the metal framework around which most microcomputers are con-          18.____
     structed?

   A.  Mainframe                          B.  Hard disk
   C.  Motherboard                        D.  Expansion slot

19.  The read/write head of a computer's disk drive is contained on the             19.____

   A.  magnetic drum                      B.  data element
   C.  token                              D.  access mechanism

20.  A(n) _____ is used to link a small computer's secondary storage device to the system.     20.____

   A.  control unit                       B.  interface board
   C.  register                           D.  buffer

21.  What processor management technique is used on most timesharing network systems?            21.____

   A.  Time-slicing                       B.  Command sorting
   C.  Apportionment                      D.  Interrupt processing

22. Which of the following procedures is used to copy data from a slow-speed device to a high-speed device for eventual input to a program?

22.____

    A. Queuing
    C. Buffing

    B. Spooling
    D. Scheduling

23. A location in memory is located by its

23.____

    A. section      B. register      C. address      D. decoder

24. _____ data is represented by a wave.

24.____

    A. Microwave      B. Digital      C. Binary      D. Analog

25. A programmer defines the logical structure of a problem by using a(n)

25.____

    A. assembler
    C. interpreter

    B. compiler
    D. nonprocedural language

---

# KEY (CORRECT ANSWERS)

| 1. | D | | 11. | C |
|----|---|---|-----|---|
| 2. | B | | 12. | B |
| 3. | A | | 13. | A |
| 4. | B | | 14. | A |
| 5. | A | | 15. | C |
| 6. | C | | 16. | B |
| 7. | D | | 17. | A |
| 8. | D | | 18. | C |
| 9. | C | | 19. | D |
| 10. | B | | 20. | B |

| 21. | A |
|-----|---|
| 22. | B |
| 23. | C |
| 24. | D |
| 25. | D |

---

# TEST 2

DIRECTIONS: Each question or incomplete statement is followed by several suggested answers or completions. Select the one that BEST answers the question or completes the statement. *PRINT THE LETTER OF THE CORRECT ANSWER IN THE SPACE AT THE RIGHT.*

1. Data is converted from digital to analog form through the process of          1.____
   - A.   demodulation
   - B.   teleporting
   - C.   cross-modulation
   - D.   modulation

2. Which of the following represents the simplest data structure?          2.____
   - A.   Record
   - B.   File
   - C.   List
   - D.   Directory

3. The term for a set of parallel wires used to transmit data, commands, or power is          3.____
   - A.   bus
   - B.   cabling
   - C.   line
   - D.   twisted pair

4. _____ limit the number of peripherals that can be linked to a microcomputer system.          4.____
   - A.   Channels
   - B.   Bus lines
   - C.   Buffers
   - D.   Slots

5. A data structure in which memory is allocated as a series of numbered cells is a(n)          5.____
   - A.   array
   - B.   block
   - C.   record
   - D.   register

6. On a disk, each program's name and location can be located on the          6.____
   - A.   index
   - B.   address
   - C.   label
   - D.   register

7. Onto which of the following structures is a processing chip stored?          7.____
   - A.   Board
   - B.   Plate
   - C.   Bus
   - D.   Disk

8. Two or more independent processors can share the same memory under a system known as          8.____
   - A.   time-sharing
   - B.   FAT binaries
   - C.   multitasking
   - D.   multiprocessing

9. A _____ is the basic storage unit around which a microcomputer system is designed.          9.____
   - A.   bit
   - B.   block
   - C.   word
   - D.   byte

10. A user communicates with an operating system by means of a(n)          10.____
   - A.   interface
   - B.   peripheral
   - C.   command language
   - D.   application

11. A _____ is used to convert data from pulse form to wave form and back again.          11.____
   - A.   channel
   - B.   modem
   - C.   SCSI port
   - D.   bus

12. Data values can be accessed according to their element numbers in a(n)          12.____
   - A.   list
   - B.   register
   - C.   record
   - D.   array

13. Under a _____ memory management scheme, a program is allocated as much memory as it needs.

    A. sector-oriented                 B. dynamic
    C. block-oriented               D. fixed partition

13.____

14. What is the term for the process of removing errors from a program?

    A. Compiling                   B. Debugging
    C. Troubleshooting             D. Extraction

14.____

15. _____ is the term for the time during which a desired sector of a disk approaches the access device.

    A. Run time                  B. Rotational delay
    C. Seek time                 D. Access time

15.____

16. What is the term for the process by which a networked computer selects the terminal it will communicate with?

    A. Compiling                   B. Polling
    C. Interfacing                 D. Selection

16.____

17. After compilers and assemblers read a programmer's code, they generate a(n)

    A. object module              B. nonprocedural language
    C. subroutine                 D. load module

17.____

18. Memory that loses its content when the machine's power is turned off is described as

    A. read-only                   B. redundant
    C. dependent                 D. volatile

18.____

19. Which module of an operating system sends primitive commands to a disk drive?

    A. Motherboard              B. IOCS
    C. CPU                     D. Command processor

19.____

20. The BASIC measure of data communications speed is

    A. bit rate                     B. baud rate
    C. kilobytes per second        D. bits per second

20.____

21. The term _____ is used to denote a single, meaningful data element, such as a person's telephone number.

    A. field       B. item       C. record       D. file

21.____

22. What is the term for the machine-level translation of a programmer's source code?

    A. Load module             B. Subroutine
    C. Source library           D. Object module

22.____

23. Which part of an instruction directs the actions of the processor?

    A. Pulse                     B. Operation code
    C. Statement                 D. Operand

23.____

24. A _____ is used to store programs that enter a multiprogramming system.

    A. tape       B. spool       C. buffer       D. queue

24.____

25. _____ is a device used to avoid data dependency and redundancy.                                    25.____

    A.  Sequential filing                 B.  Continuous backup
    C.  Random filing                     D.  Database

---

# KEY (CORRECT ANSWERS)

| 1. | A | | 11. | B |
|----|---|---|-----|---|
| 2. | C | | 12. | D |
| 3. | A | | 13. | B |
| 4. | D | | 14. | B |
| 5. | A | | 15. | B |
| | | | | |
| 6. | A | | 16. | B |
| 7. | A | | 17. | A |
| 8. | D | | 18. | D |
| 9. | C | | 19. | B |
| 10. | C | | 20. | B |

| 21. | A |
|-----|---|
| 22. | D |
| 23. | B |
| 24. | D |
| 25. | D |

---

# EXAMINATION SECTION
# TEST 1

DIRECTIONS: Each question or incomplete statement is followed by several suggested answers or completions. Select the one that BEST answers the question or completes the statement. *PRINT THE LETTER OF THE CORRECT ANSWER IN THE SPACE AT THE RIGHT.*

1. A track and a sector number on a disk combine to form a(n)　　　　　　1.＿＿＿

    A. register　　　　B. byte　　　　C. address　　　　D. file name

2. A(n) ＿＿＿＿＿ microcomputer system design focuses on what must be done, but not on how to do it.　　2.＿＿＿

    A. logical　　　　B. listed　　　　C. protocol　　　　D. objective

3. An instruction is retrieved from main memory by the ＿＿＿＿＿ processor component.　　3.＿＿＿

    A. arithmetic and logic unit　　　　B. instruction counter
    C. register　　　　D. instruction control unit

4. What is the term for a support program that reads a source program, translates the source statements to machine language, and outputs a complete binary object program?　　4.＿＿＿

    A. Scheduler　　　　B. Interpreter　　　　C. Compiler　　　　D. Assembler

5. A(n) ＿＿＿＿＿ is composed of a group of related data records.　　5.＿＿＿

    A. array　　　　B. list　　　　C. directory　　　　D. file

6. What is the term for an extra bit added to data bits that will allow a computer to check the bit pattern for accuracy?　　6.＿＿＿

    A. End code　　　　B. Bit stuffer
    C. Operand　　　　D. Parity bit

7. When disks are stacked into a pack, what is the term for the set of tracks accessed by the access device?　　7.＿＿＿

    A. Block　　　　B. Sector　　　　C. Cylinder　　　　D. Drum

8. Any data communications medium can be described by the generic term　　8.＿＿＿

    A. line　　　　B. port　　　　C. converter　　　　D. modem

9. The operating systems of most microcomputers are driven by　　9.＿＿＿

    A. commands　　　　B. hardware
    C. software　　　　D. a control unit

10. What is the term for a complete machine-level program that is in a form ready to be placed into main memory and executed?　　10.＿＿＿

    A. Load module　　　　B. Object module
    C. Schedule　　　　D. Compiler

11. A programmer writes one instruction for each machine-level instruction when using a(n)    11.____

    A.  generator                      B.  assembler
    C.  resource fork               D.  compiler

12. A binary digit is represented by a    12.____

    A.  byte         B.  code         C.  bit         D.  buffer

13. Which module of the operating system is responsible for communicating with input and    13.____
output devices?

    A.  Command processor         B.  Boot
    C.  IOCS                      D.  Bus line

14. Two or more disks stacked on a common drive shaft are known as a    14.____

    A.  pack                      B.  roll-out
    C.  multidrive               D.  cylinder

15. The _____ of an operating system loads programs into main memory.    15.____

    A.  compiler                   B.  processor manager
    C.  scheduler                D.  assembler

16. A _____ can be used to synchronize devices or media that operate at different speeds.    16.____

    A.  buffer         B.  spooler         C.  modem         D.  protocol

17. The part of an instruction that identifies memory locations to participate in an operation is    17.____
the

    A.  pulse                     B.  statement
    C.  operand                 D.  operation code

18. What is the term for a support program that reads a single source statement, translates    18.____
the statement to machine language, executes the instructions, and then moves onto the
next source statement?

    A.  Scheduler                B.  Interpreter
    C.  Compiler               D.  Assembler

19. _____ is used to link a computer's internal components.    19.____

    A.  Cables                   B.  Bus lines
    C.  Clock pulses            D.  Motherboard

20. Data are transferred from main memory to a disk's surface in units called    20.____

    A.  sectors        B.  blocks       C.  tracks       D.  words

21. Under a _____ memory management scheme, programs are stored on disk, with only    21.____
active portions stored into memory.

    A.  virtual                    B.  dynamic
    C.  block-oriented         D.  fixed partition

22. A(n) _____ is composed of a group of related data fields.  22.____

    A.  array        B.  list        C.  record        D.  file

23. Which of the following serves to allocate a processor's time?  23.____

    A.  User                         B.  Bus
    C.  Operating system        D.  Motherboard

24. On a disk, the address of the beginning of each program is stored on the  24.____

    A.  tree        B.  block        C.  index        D.  register

25. A program's steps are divided into units of  25.____

    A.  code                       B.  commands
    C.  sectors                    D.  instructions

-------

# KEY (CORRECT ANSWERS)

| | | | | |
|---|---|---|---|---|
| 1. | C | | 11. | B |
| 2. | A | | 12. | C |
| 3. | D | | 13. | C |
| 4. | C | | 14. | A |
| 5. | D | | 15. | C |
| 6. | D | | 16. | A |
| 7. | C | | 17. | C |
| 8. | A | | 18. | B |
| 9. | A | | 19. | B |
| 10. | A | | 20. | A |

21. A
22. C
23. C
24. C
25. D

-------

# TEST 2

DIRECTIONS:   Each question or incomplete statement is followed by several suggested answers or completions. Select the one that BEST answers the question or completes the statement. *PRINT THE LETTER OF THE CORRECT ANSWER IN THE SPACE AT THE RIGHT.*

1.   The address of the next instruction to be executed is held in the _____ processor component.

   A.   main memory
   B.   register
   C.   arithmetic and logic unit
   D.   instruction control unit

1.____

2.   What is the term for an electronic signal that is part of a protocol?

   A.   Token          B.   Reach          C.   Chord          D.   Pulse

2.____

3.   Under _____ processing, data records are processed in the order in which they are recorded.

   A.   continuous          B.   consecutive
   C.   serial              D.   sequential

3.____

4.   _____ processing is a computer application in which data are collected over time and then processed together.

   A.   Transaction          B.   Cumulative
   C.   Batch                D.   Continuous

4.____

5.   A(n) _____ serves as a hardware/software interface.

   A.   buffer              B.   application
   C.   operating system    D.   bus

5.____

6.   Any connection for an electronic communication line can be called a(n)

   A.   port          B.   poll          C.   line          D.   front end

6.____

7.   During a single machine cycle, a processor retrieves and executes

   A.   one command
   B.   one instruction
   C.   at least two statements
   D.   at least two instructions

7.____

8.   A _____ is NOT an example of a data structure.

   A.   record          B.   file          C.   list          D.   directory

8.____

9.   Which of the following serves to translate a computer's internal codes and a peripheral device's external codes?

   A.   Buffer              B.   RAM
   C.   Interface           D.   Encoder/decoder

9.____

10. Which of the following is the memory management scheme MOST often used with time-shared systems?    10.____

    A. Pages
    C. Fixed partitions
    B. Roll-in/roll-out
    D. First-come/first-serve

11. When the same data are recorded in two or more files, _____ has occurred.    11.____

    A. redundancy
    C. backup
    B. leakage
    D. loss

12. For a batch processing application, a _____ file organization should be selected.    12.____

    A. sequential
    C. direct
    B. indexed
    D. random

13. If a bus line transmits bits one by one, it is described as a _____ line.    13.____

    A. serial
    C. continuous
    B. consecutive
    D. parallel

14. Data is converted from analog to digital form through the process of    14.____

    A. demodulation
    C. cross-modulation
    B. data flow
    D. modulation

15. A _____ loads a computer's operating system.    15.____

    A. program loader
    C. command processor
    B. IOCS
    D. boot

16. Which of the following differentiates a computer from a calculator?    16.____

    A. Memory
    C. A processor
    B. Input
    D. A stored program

17. Which element of a microcomputer system will devote a separate unit to suit each peripheral?    17.____

    A. Bus
    C. Motherboard
    B. Channel
    D. Interface

18. What is the term for the interference that distorts electronic signals transmitted over a distance?    18.____

    A. Ghosting
    C. Static
    B. Noise
    D. Interference

19. By responding to a(n) _____, an operating system can switch from program to program.    19.____

    A. operand
    C. interrupter
    B. user
    D. program

20. If a microcomputer system's memory capacity is adjusted, the result will be a change in    20.____

    A. word size
    C. precision
    B. processing speed
    D. seek time

21. A _____ generates the regular electronic pulses that drive a computer.　　21.____

    A. clock        B. IOCS        C. bus        D. processor

22. Under what type of access can data records be accessed in any order?　　22.____

    A. Serial                    B. Random
    C. Direct                    D. Sequential

23. A _____ is a brief message printed or displayed by a program or the operating system　　23.____
that asks the user for input.

    A. token        B. seek        C. protocol        D. prompt

24. Data on a disk are recorded in a series of concentric circles called　　24.____

    A. blocks        B. tracks        C. cycles        D. sectors

25. What is the term for a programming language in which one mnemonic source statement　　25.____
is coded for each machine-level instruction?

    A. Scheduler               B. Interpreter
    C. Compiler               D. Assembler

---

# KEY (CORRECT ANSWERS)

| | | | | |
|---|---|---|---|---|
| 1. | B | | 11. | A |
| 2. | A | | 12. | A |
| 3. | D | | 13. | A |
| 4. | C | | 14. | D |
| 5. | C | | 15. | D |
| 6. | A | | 16. | D |
| 7. | B | | 17. | D |
| 8. | D | | 18. | B |
| 9. | C | | 19. | C |
| 10. | B | | 20. | B |

| | |
|---|---|
| 21. | A |
| 22. | C |
| 23. | D |
| 24. | B |
| 25. | D |

---

# EXAMINATION SECTION

# TEST 1

DIRECTIONS: Each question or incomplete statement is followed by several suggested answers or completions. Select the one that BEST answers the question or completes the statement. *PRINT THE LETTER OF THE CORRECT ANSWER IN THE SPACE AT THE RIGHT.*

1. A spreadsheet program is NOT used for

    A. determining averages
    B. scheduling
    C. writing reports
    D. estimating job costs

1.____

2. In order to write-protect a 3.5" floppy disk, a user must

    A. cover the write-protect notch
    B. move the write-protect tab down, leaving an opening in the corner of the disk
    C. cover the recording window
    D. immobilize the shutter mechanism

2.____

3. Which of the following is a mathematical function of a spreadsheet program?

    A. Averages
    B. Logarithms
    C. Standard deviation
    D. Maximum/minimum values

3.____

4. The purpose of a device driver is to

    A. tell hardware devices precisely how to perform their jobs
    B. manage the movement of a read/write head over a hard disk drive
    C. facilitate the I/O interface
    D. manage the movement of a read/write head over a floppy disk

4.____

5. Each of the following is a purpose that is typically served with a desktop publishing program EXCEPT

    A. printing newsletters
    B. illustrating manuals
    C. creating flyers
    D. printing menus

5.____

6. Which of the following is an operating system that relies on icon selection or menu options to select commands?

    A. OS/2      B. Unix      C. MS-DOS      D. Windows

6.____

7. Typically, the quality of a printer is expressed in terms of

7.____

A. resolution
B. RAM
C. DPI
D. pixellation

8. Which of the following is a purpose that can be served by a database program?   8._____

    A. Balancing accounts
    B. Illustrating manuals
    C. Keeping track of schedules
    D. Generating client reports

9. What type of adapter would be required if a user wanted to upgrade the graphics capabil-   9._____
ity of a computer monitor to a maximum number of 256 possible colors?

    A. XGA      B. CGA      C. VGA      D. SVG

10. Which of the following is a statistical function of a spreadsheet program?   10._____

    A. Maximum/minimum values
    B. Logarithms
    C. Absolute values
    D. Compounding periods

11. For which of the following functions would a flat-file database be MOST useful?   11._____

    A. Compiling invoices
    B. Creating a graph based on stored sales figures
    C. Storing information to print mailing labels
    D. Calculating inventory

12. Data in electronic spreadsheets are stored in areas called   12._____

    A. records
    B. cells
    C. plug-ins
    D. fields

13. If a user on a network wants to receive information from a host computer, he/she would   13._____
have to_____the desired files.

    A. uplink
    B. translate
    C. write a call program for
    D. download

14. A_____is an optical storage device.   14._____

    A. video buffer
    B. floppy disk
    C. CD-ROM
    D. magnetic tape

15. Each of the following is a function served by a utility program EXCEPT          15.____

    A. removing viruses
    B. setting alarms
    C. creating reports
    D. creating menus

Questions 16 through 25 concern the DOS command-driven environment. For the purpose stated next to each number, choose the command that would need to be typed next to the prompt on a user's computer screen.

16. To find out what's stored on a disk, type          16.____

    A. ver        B. dir        C. list        D. cd

17. To clear the display screen, type          17.____

    A. ren        B. chkdsk        C. clear        D. cls

18. To create a directory or subdirectory, type          18.____

    A. md        B. rd        C. ren        D. new

19. To display the version number of the installed DOS, type          19.____

    A. type        B. DOStype        C. format        D. ver

20. To delete a directory or subdirectory, type          20.____

    A. del        B. md        C. rd        D. delete

21. To prepare a hard disk for formatting, type          21.____

    A. format        B. fdisk        C. chkdisk        D. rd

22. To list the contents of an ASCII file on screen, type          22.____

    A. file        B. list        C. type        D. asc

23. To copy a file or directory, type          23.____

    A. xcopy        B. file/dir        C. copy        D. diskcopy

24. To rename a file, type          24.____

    A. name        B. cd        C. rest        D. ren

25. To delete a directory, type          25.____

    A. rmdir        B. cd        C. del        D. deldir

# KEY (CORRECT ANSWERS)

| | | | |
|---|---|---|---|
| 1. | C | 11. | C |
| 2. | B | 12. | B |
| 3. | B | 13. | D |
| 4. | A | 14. | C |
| 5. | B | 15. | C |
| 6. | A | 16. | B |
| 7. | C | 17. | D |
| 8. | D | 18. | A |
| 9. | D | 19. | D |
| 10. | A | 20. | C |

| | |
|---|---|
| 21. | B |
| 22. | C |
| 23. | A |
| 24. | D |
| 25. | A |

# TEST 2

DIRECTIONS:  Each question or incomplete statement is followed by several suggested answers or completions. Select the one that BEST answers the question or completes the statement. *PRINT THE LETTER OF THE CORRECT ANSWER IN THE SPACE AT THE RIGHT.*

NOTE: The questions on this test concern Macintosh applications.

1.  Mac users can find the amount of space available on a disk                1.____

    A.  in the upper right-hand corner of the disk window
    B.  by consulting the System file
    C.  by keying command-M
    D.  only by using the Get Info command under a File menu

2.  The simplest way for a user to make a copy of a file into another folder on the same disk    2.____
    is to

    A.  select the file, then choose *duplicate* from the file menu
    B.  hold down the option key as the file is dragged into the folder
    C.  select the file and press command-D
    D.  make a copy onto a floppy disk and then drag that copy back onto the hard disk

3.  When a user drags a file from the hard disk to a floppy disk, the user is        3.____

    A.  moving the file from the hard disk to the floppy disk
    B.  making a copy of the file for the hard disk
    C.  making a copy of the file onto the floppy disk
    D.  deleting the file

4.  When printing to a new printer for the first time, which of the following should be per-    4.____
    formed FIRST?

    A.  Choose the printer driver
    B.  Choose the name of the printer
    C.  Select *Chooser* from the Apple or File menu
    D.  Click the setup button or choose Auto Setup

5.  When using a mouse to select an icon, which of the following actions is necessary?    5.____

    A.  Single-click                    B.  Double-click
    C.  Press                           D.  Press and drag

6.  When using a mouse to see what's in a menu, which of the following actions is neces-    6.____
    sary?

    A.  Single-click                    B.  Double-click
    C.  Press                           D.  Press and drag

7.  When using a mouse to open a file, you should                            7.____

    A.  single-click                    B.  double-click
    C.  press                           D.  press and drag

8.  What is the keyboard shortcut for closing a window displayed on the desktop?    8._____

    A.  Command-W
    B.  Control-Option-E
    C.  Command-C
    D.  Command-O

9.  When the *Save As* dialog box is on the desktop, what is the visual cue that the displayed    9._____
    list has been selected?

    A.  All file names appear in gray
    B.  A flashing insertion point
    C.  Folder names appear in black
    D.  A double border around the list

10. In any text environment, pressing the delete key will cause the_____ to back up a    10._____
    space.

    A.  finder                        B.  I-beam
    C.  insertion point               D.  pointer

11. The keyboard shortcut for pasting text is Command-_____.    11._____

    A.  V            B.  X            C.  B            D.  C

12. Which control panel would be used to change the size of the type of the windows on the    12._____
    desktop?

    A.  General Controls
    B.  Views
    C.  Monitors
    D.  Labels

13. Which control panel would be adjusted to display fewer colors on the monitor in order to    13._____
    save memory?

    A.  ColorSync                     B.  Views
    C.  Monitors                      D.  Labels

14. If a real file is thrown away by a user, its aliases will    14._____

    A.  remain unaffected
    B.  be deleted also
    C.  remain but may only provide access to text files
    D.  remain on the disk but will not provide access to anything

15. In any set of buttons on the desktop, the default button will    15._____

    A.  be bordered in gray
    B.  be lettered in gray
    C.  have a thick double border
    D.  be lettered in black

16. Whenever a menu item is followed by an ellipsis (...), the selection of that item will produce a(n)

    A. opened file
    B. dialog box
    C. opened application
    D. choice among listed Control Panels

16.____

17. When a set of options appear with checkbox buttons next to them, this is a clue that

    A. a submenu will be produced by clicking a button
    B. any number of buttons may be selected or deselected in combination
    C. clicking a button will not produce any changes until the computer is restarted
    D. only one of the buttons may be selected at a time

17.____

18. If a disk's, folder's or application's icon appears gray, it is a sign that the item

    A. that created it cannot be found
    B. is about to have its name changed
    C. is already open
    D. has been deleted from the RAM

18.____

19. If a document icon is blank, it is probably a sign that

    A. it has already been opened
    B. the application that created it has already been opened
    C. it has been deleted
    D. the application that created the document cannot be found on the disk

19.____

20. If a scroll bar in a window or dialog box appears gray, it is a sign that

    A. there are other items in the window that are not currently visible
    B. the display needs vertical centering
    C. the scroll box is not available
    D. the display needs horizontal centering

20.____

21. What is the keyboard shortcut for creating a new folder?

    A. Command-W
    B. Command-F
    C. Command-N
    D. Control-Option-F

21.____

22. What is the visual clue that the name of a file, folder or disk on the desktop is about to be changed?

    A. A border has appeared around the name
    B. The entire icon is highlighted
    C. The name is highlighted
    D. The entire icon is gray

22.____

23. To print the contents of an entire screen, a user should

    A. choose *Print* from the file menu while running an application
    B. choose *Print Desktop* from the file menu

23.____

C. press Command-P
D. choose *Print Window* from the file menu

24. When the *Save As* dialog box is on the desktop, what should a user do to select the edit     24._____
box for input?

    A. Press the Tab key
    B. Click on the *Save* button
    C. Press the Shift key
    D. Press Command-S

25. To put files back where they came from, a user should     25._____

    A. drag the file into the System folder while the *Fast Find* Apple menu is running
    B. press Command-W
    C. create an alias
    D. press Command-Y

_____

# KEY (CORRECT ANSWERS)

| | | | | |
|---|---|---|---|---|
| 1. | A | | 11. | A |
| 2. | B | | 12. | B |
| 3. | C | | 13. | C |
| 4. | C | | 14. | D |
| 5. | A | | 15. | C |
| | | | | |
| 6. | C | | 16. | B |
| 7. | B | | 17. | B |
| 8. | A | | 18. | C |
| 9. | D | | 19. | D |
| 10. | C | | 20. | A |

| | |
|---|---|
| 21. | C |
| 22. | A |
| 23. | B |
| 24. | A |
| 25. | D |

_____

# EXAMINATION SECTION
## TEST 1

DIRECTIONS: Each question or incomplete statement is followed by several suggested answers or completions. Select the one that BEST answers the question or completes the statement. *PRINT THE LETTER OF THE CORRECT ANSWER IN THE SPACE AT THE RIGHT.*

1. A microprocessor includes media for each of the following EXCEPT          1._____

    A. secondary storage          B. control
    C. logic                   D. memory

2. Which of the following protocols is LEAST likely to be used in a wide–area network          2._____
(WAN)?

    A. SNA             B. Token passing
    C. TCP/IP          D. DEC DNA

3. In an expert system, the rule base is sometimes searched using a strategy that begins          3._____
with a hypothesis and seeks out more information until the hypothesis is either proved or
disproved. This strategy is known as

    A. backward chaining
    B. key fielding
    C. indexed sequential access
    D. process specification

4. The meaning of signs, symbols, messages or systems are involved in a body of inquiry          4._____
known as

    A. linguistics         B. semantics
    C. communications   D. syntactics

5. Which of the following is a query language?          5._____

    A. Nomad       B. Ideal       C. Systat       D. RPG–III

6. Which of the following is the typical unit of measurement used by systems designers to          6._____
estimate the length of time needed to complete a project?

    A. Data–week       B. Man–hour
    C. File–hour        D. Man–month

7. Which of the following is the oldest professional computer society in the United States?          7._____

    A. Data Processing Management Association (DPMA)
    B. Institute for Certification of Computer Professionals (ICP)
    C. Association of Computing Machinery (ACM)
    D. Information Technology Association of America (ITAA)

8. Which of the following terms is commonly used to describe the interaction of people and          8._____
machines in the work environment, especially in terms of job design and health issues?

    A. Connectivity       B. Ergonomics
    C. Feasibility        D. Interface

9. Which of the following is a likely application of the sensitivity analysis models of a decision–support system?    9.____

   A. Forecasting sales
   B. Determining the proper product mix within a given market
   C. Predicting the actions of competitors
   D. Goal seeking

10. What is the term for the temporary storage location in a control unit where small amounts of data or instructions reside for thousandths of a second just before use?    10.____

   A. Cache      B. Register      C. Sector      D. Buffer

11. Systems whose behavior includes options without specification of probabilities within the system are described as    11.____

   A. runaway             B. possibilistic
   C. stochastic          D. probabilistic

12. The physical devices and software that link various hardware components and transfer data from one physical location to another are known collectively as    12.____

   A. cyberspace
   B. wide–area networks
   C. telecommunications technology
   D. semantic networks

13. Which of the following is a tangible benefit associated with organizational information systems?    13.____

   A. Streamlined operations      B. Higher asset utilization
   C. Inventory reduction          D. Improved planning

14. Which of the following is NOT generally considered to be a physical component of an MIS?    14.____

   A. Personnel           B. Information
   C. Procedures         D. Software

15. Any undesired information in a communication channel which is not part of the intended message is typically referred to as    15.____

   A. resistance          B. noise
   C. data error          D. cross–talk

16. Which of the following is the ASCII 8–bit binary code for the number 1?    16.____

   A. 0001 0001        B. 0101 0001
   C. 0000 1000        D. 1001 0001

17. Which of the following is a method of organizing expert system knowledge into chunks in which relationships are based on shared characteristics determined by the user?    17.____

   A. Indexing          B. GUI
   C. Batch processing     D. Frames

18. Which of the following is a telecommunications requirement that is particular to the task of on–line data entry?

    A. High–capacity video and data capabilities
    B. Infrequent, high–volume bursts of information
    C. Instant response
    D. Direct response

18.____

19. What is the term for the technology which breaks blocks of text into small fixed bundles of data and routes them in an economical way through an available communications channel?

    A. Optical character recognition
    B. Frame relay
    C. Packet switching
    D. Branch exchange

19.____

20. A transaction processing system rejects a transaction on the basis that it includes a Social Security number which contains an alphabetic character. This is an example of a(n) _____ check.

    A. reasonableness
    B. format
    C. dependency
    D. existence

20.____

21. The smallest unit of data for defining an image in a computer is the

    A. byte
    B. pixel
    C. quark
    D. bit

21.____

22. In a microcomputer, which of the following transmits signals specifying whether to read or write data from a given primary storage address, input device, or output device?

    A. Control bus
    B. Address bus
    C. Data bus
    D. CPU

22.____

23. Which of the following stages occurs the LATEST in the traditional systems life cycle model?

    A. Systems study
    B. Programming
    C. Design
    D. Project definition

23.____

24. The fastest and most expensive memory used in a microcomputer is located in the

    A. cache
    B. register
    C. hard disk
    D. RAM

24.____

25. Which of the following is an optical disk system that allows users to record data only once, but to read the data indefinitely?

    A. WORM
    B. EPROM
    C. RAM
    D. TQM

25.____

# KEY (CORRECT ANSWERS)

| | | | | |
|---|---|---|---|---|
| 1. | A | | 11. | B |
| 2. | B | | 12. | C |
| 3. | A | | 13. | C |
| 4. | B | | 14. | B |
| 5. | D | | 15. | B |
| | | | | |
| 6. | D | | 16. | B |
| 7. | C | | 17. | D |
| 8. | B | | 18. | D |
| 9. | D | | 19. | C |
| 10. | B | | 20. | B |

| | |
|---|---|
| 21. | B |
| 22. | A |
| 23. | B |
| 24. | B |
| 25. | A |

# TEST 2

DIRECTIONS: Each question or incomplete statement is followed by several suggested answers or completions. Select the one that BEST answers the question or completes the statement. *PRINT THE LETTER OF THE CORRECT ANSWER IN THE SPACE AT THE RIGHT.*

1. Which of the following styles of systems development is most often used for information systems at the individual level?

    A. End–user computing
    B. Commercial software packages
    C. Prototyping
    D. Traditional life cycle

1._____

2. Which of the following is a programming language that was developed in 1956 for scientific and mathematical applications?

    A. COBOL      B. BASIC      C. Pascal      D. FORTRAN

2._____

3. Which of the following personnel would be considered a *technical specialist* in an MIS department?

    A. Education specialist      B. Database administrator
    C. Applications programmer      D. Systems analyst

3._____

4. Which of the following is NOT a characteristic of a fault–tolerant system?

    A. The use of special software routines to detect hardware failures
    B. Extra memory chips, processors, and disk storage
    C. Continuous detection of bugs or program defects
    D. Hardware parts that can be removed without system disruption

4._____

5. Defining a system program in such a way that it may call itself is an example of

    A. eudemony      B. recursion
    C. redundancy      D. artificial intelligence

5._____

6. What is the term used to enumerate the number of bits that can be processed at one time by a computer?

    A. Data bus width      B. Word length
    C. RAM capacity      D. Bandwidth

6._____

7. Which of the following is another term for a field, or a grouping of characters into a word, group of words, or complete number?

    A. Code      B. Byte
    C. Data element      D. File

7._____

8. A person in a multi–user system sends a message using the OSI model to another user at a different location. At the messenger's end of the system, after passing through the *session* layer of the model, the message will then enter the _____ layer.

    A. transport      B. network
    C. presentation      D. data link

8._____

9. Which of the following is NOT a disadvantage associated with the traditional life cycle model of systems development?

   A. Time consumption          B. Oversimplification
   C. Cost                       D. Inflexibility

9.____

10. Transmission speeds that would fall within the expected range of coaxial cable are _____ per second.

   A. 400 bits                B. 50 megabits
   C. 300 megabits         D. 7 gigabits

10.____

11. Which of the following is a telecommunications computer that collects and temporarily stores messages from terminals for batch transmission to the host computer?

   A. Assembler            B. Concentrator
   C. Buffer                 D. Compiler

11.____

12. Which of the following is an advantage associated with the centralized or teleprocessing model of multi–user systems?

   A. Local computing       B. Scaleability
   C. Low start–up costs    D. Low technical risk

12.____

13. Software systems that can operate on different hardware platforms are referred to as _____ systems.

   A. open                  B. interoperable
   C. branched            D. transmigrational

13.____

14. What is the term for the process by which the properties of a collection (i.e., of data) are described in terms of the sums of the properties of the units contained in the collection?

   A. Unity                B. Autarky
   C. Chunking           D. Aggregation

14.____

15. In systems terminology, what is the term for output that is returned to the appropriate members of an organization to help them evaluate or correct input?

   A. Exit data            B. Feedback
   C. Assessor           D. Valuation

15.____

16. The years 1957 to 1963 are generally considered to have been the _____ generation in the evolution of computer hardware technology.

   A. first      B. second      C. third      D. fourth

16.____

17. A conversion approach in which the new system completely replaces the old one on an appointed day is known as

   A. focused differentiation   B. direct cutover
   C. allied distribution      D. batch processing

17.____

18. Of the following types of business network redesign, the one that can be said to be most highly coupled is/are    18.____

    A.  interenterprise system access
    B.  knowledge networks
    C.  EDI
    D.  interenterprise process integration

19. Which of the following terms is used to describe the shape or configuration of a telecommunications network?    19.____

    A.  Duplex               B.  Topology
    C.  Protocol            D.  Transmissivity

20. Which of the following is/are recognized differences between microcomputers and workstations?    20.____

    I.   Microcomputers have more powerful mathematical processing capabilities.
    II.  Microcomputers are more useful for computer–aided design (CAD).
    III.  Workstations are more widely used by knowledge workers.
    IV.  Workstations can more easily perform multiple tasks simultaneously.

The CORRECT answer is:

    A.  I, II        B.  II, III        C.  III, IV        D.  II, IV

21. Which of the following signifies a tool for retrieving and transferring files from a remote computer?    21.____

    A.  EDI        B.  CPU        C.  TCP/IP        D.  FTP

22. Which of the following is a federal privacy law that applies to private institutions?    22.____

    A.  Freedom of Information Act of 1968 (as amended)
    B.  Privacy Act of 1974 (as amended)
    C.  Privacy Protection Act of 1980
    D.  Computer Matching and Privacy Protection Act of 1988

23. The main contribution of end–user systems development typically occurs in the area of    23.____

    A.  productivity enhancement
    B.  improved updating functions
    C.  increased technical complexity
    D.  improved efficiency in transaction processing

24. In cooperative processing, a mainframe and a microcomputer generally share tasks. The mainframe, however, is generally best at performing    24.____

    A.  screen presentation        B.  error processing
    C.  data field editing         D.  file input and output

25. In a systems development process, users are made active members of development project teams, and some users are placed in charge of system training and installation. In this case, management has made use of _____ tools.        25.____

    A.  external integration        B.  internal integration
    C.  formal planning             D.  formal control

---

# KEY (CORRECT ANSWERS)

| | | | |
|---|---|---|---|
| 1. | C | 11. | B |
| 2. | D | 12. | D |
| 3. | B | 13. | A |
| 4. | C | 14. | D |
| 5. | B | 15. | B |
| 6. | B | 16. | B |
| 7. | C | 17. | B |
| 8. | A | 18. | B |
| 9. | B | 19. | B |
| 10. | B | 20. | C |

21. D
22. C
23. A
24. D
25. A

---

# TEST 3

DIRECTIONS: Each question or incomplete statement is followed by several suggested answers or completions. Select the one that BEST answers the question or completes the statement. *PRINT THE LETTER OF THE CORRECT ANSWER IN THE SPACE AT THE RIGHT.*

1. As a general rule, the development of a system that will be used by others can be expected to take_____ as long as the development of an individual system that will be used only by the developer.

    A. half
    C. three times
    B. twice
    D. five times

    1.____

2. In LANs, the token ring configuration is most useful for

    A. broadcasting messages to the entire network through a single circuit
    B. multidirectional transmissions between microcomputers or between micros and a larger computer
    C. transmissions between microcomputers and a larger computer that require a degree of traffic control
    D. transmitting large volumes of data between microcomputers

    2.____

3. Which of the following statements about expert systems is generally TRUE? They

    A. function best in lower–level clerical functions
    B. require minimal development resources
    C. are highly adaptable over time
    D. are capable of representing a wide range of causal models

    3.____

4. A middle–range machine with a RAM capacity that measures from about 10 megabytes to over 1 gigabyte is known as a

    A. microcomputer
    C. desktop computer
    B. minicomputer
    D. mainframe

    4.____

5. Which of the following media uses the sector method for storing data?

    A. Cache
    C. Hard disk
    B. Floppy disk
    D. CD–ROM

    5.____

6. When mechanisms of functional subsystems are connected causally to influence each other, they are said to be

    A. aggregated
    C. synchronous
    B. coupled
    D. constrained

    6.____

7. Which of the following storage media generally has the largest capacity?

    A. Cache
    C. Optical disk
    B. Magnetic disk
    D. Magnetic tape

    7.____

8. In terms of information ethics, the mechanisms for assessing responsibility for decisions and actions are referred to as

    A. liability
    C. creditability
    B. capacity
    D. accountability

    8.____

9. Which of the following signifies the central switching system that handles a firm's voice and digital communications?

    A.  OSI           B.  DSS           C.  PBX           D.  LAN

9.____

10. What is the term for the LAN channel technology that provides a single path for transmitting text, graphics, voice, or video data at one time?

    A.  Bus                        B.  Baseband
    C.  Firewall                 D.  Broadband

10.____

11. The stage in a system's life cycle in which testing, training, and conversion occur is termed

    A.  evaluation               B.  design
    C.  installation            D.  documentation

11.____

12. Which of the following is NOT a type of processor used in telecommunications systems?

    A.  Coaxial cable          B.  Controller
    C.  Modem                 D.  Multiplexer

12.____

13. A database that is stored in more than one physical location is described as

    A.  sequential              B.  wide–area
    C.  distributed            D.  indexed

13.____

14. An organization decides to redesign its information system using only the components that are already available to it. In the language of systems theory, the resulting system would be described as a(n)

    A.  ensemble      B.  creod        C.  kluge       D.  cyborg

14.____

15. What is the term for an integrated circuit made by printing thousands or millions of transistors on a small silicon chip?

    A.  Cache                B.  Semiconductor
    C.  Control unit          D.  Microprocessor

15.____

16. Computer programming includes a logic pattern that allows for the repetition of certain actions while a specified condition occurs or until a certain conditions exists. This pattern is known as the

    A.  object linkage         B.  selection construct
    C.  key field             D.  iteration construct

16.____

17. Which of the following is the standard or reference model for allowing e–mail systems operating on different hardware to communicate?

    A.  X.400         B.  X.25        C.  X.12       D.  FDDI

17.____

18. Which of the following terms is used to denote circular tracks on the same vertical line within a disk pack?

    A.  Track         B.  Spindle       C.  Sector       D.  Cylinder

18.____

19. A system that is capable of listing the descriptions of each of a certain set of alternatives is described as    19.____

    A. generative
    C. smart
    B. contingency–based
    D. stochastic

20. Which of the following is an operating cost associated with an information system?    20.____

    A. Database establishment
    C. Personnel training
    B. Facilities
    D. Hardware acquisition

21. As a collaboration tool, the World Wide Web involves    21.____

    A. data that undergoes frequent updating
    B. documents predominantly authored by a single user
    C. applications with data at multiple sites
    D. applications with high security requirements

22. A mathematical formula used to translate a record's key field directly into its storage location is known as a(n) _____ algorithm.    22.____

    A. synchronous
    C. asynchronous
    B. genetic
    D. transform

23. Which of the following is a common DISADVANTAGE associated with outsourcing the systems development process?    23.____

    A. Loss of control over system function
    B. Increased costs
    C. Generally slow progress
    D. Increased paperwork requirements

24. Which of the following is a network topology in which all computers and other devices are connected to a central host computer?    24.____

    A. LAN    B. Star    C. Ring    D. Bus

25. In terms of information systems, *processing* means the    25.____

    A. assignment of data to certain categories for later use
    B. calculation or computation of data to arrive at a solution or conclusion
    C. conversion, manipulation, and analysis of raw input into a meaningful form
    D. collection or capture of raw data for use in an information system

# KEY (CORRECT ANSWERS)

| | | | | |
|---|---|---|---|---|
| 1. | C | | 11. | C |
| 2. | D | | 12. | A |
| 3. | A | | 13. | C |
| 4. | B | | 14. | C |
| 5. | B | | 15. | B |
| | | | | |
| 6. | B | | 16. | D |
| 7. | C | | 17. | A |
| 8. | D | | 18. | D |
| 9. | C | | 19. | A |
| 10. | B | | 20. | B |

| | |
|---|---|
| 21. | B |
| 22. | D |
| 23. | A |
| 24. | B |
| 25. | C |

———

# EXAMINATION SECTION
## TEST 1

DIRECTIONS: Each question or incomplete statement is followed by several suggested answers or completions. Select the one that BEST answers the question or completes the statement. *PRINT THE LETTER OF THE CORRECT ANSWER IN THE SPACE AT THE RIGHT.*

1. What is the term for the methodical simplification of a logical data model?　　　　1._____

    A. Elucidation                   B. Normalization
    C. Partitioning                D. Bit streaming

2. Systems development projects _____ are most likely to benefit from the use of internal integration tools.　　　　2._____

    A. with high levels of technical complexity
    B. in which end-user participation is voluntary
    C. which experience counterimplementation
    D. that are small in scale and involve only specific departments

3. In a typical telecommunications system, a message that has just passed through the front-end multiplexer will then pass through　　　　3._____

    A. a front-end processor         B. a modem or modems
    C. a controller               D. the host computer

4. Which of the following is a characteristic of data warehouse data? They　　　　4._____

    A. are organized from a functional view
    B. are volatile to support operations within a company
    C. include enterprise-wide data, collected from legacy systems
    D. involve individual fields that may be inconsistent across the enterprise

5. Which of the following terms is used to enumerate the bits that can be moved at one time between a CPU, primary storage, and other devices of a computer?　　　　5._____

    A. Bandwidth                 B. RAM cache
    C. Data bus width            D. Register

6. In enterprise analysis, data elements are organized into groups that support related sets of organizational processes. These groups are known as　　　　6._____

    A. data sub-units            B. critical success factors
    C. end-user interfaces        D. logical application groups

7. Which of the following terms is used to describe a system's order of complexity?　　　　7._____

    A. Resilience                B. Eudemony
    C. Ordinality               D. Dialectics

8. Of the following file organization methods, the only one that can be used on magnetic tape is　　　　8._____

    A. random                   B. indexed sequential
    C. alphabetic              D. sequential

9. What is the term for a set of rules and procedures that govern transmissions between the components of a telecommunications network?  9._____

    A. Criteria                 B. Norms
    C. Algorithms            D. Protocols

10. In what type of processing can more than one instruction be processed at once, by breaking down a problem into smaller parts and processing them simultaneously?  10._____

    A. Parallel              B. Indexed
    C. Sequential          D. Batch

11. Which of the following terms is used to describe a system in which the internal parameters can be changed when necessary through feedback?  11._____

    A. Homeostatic         B. Elastic
    C. Capacitive          D. Heuristic

12. Each of the following is a rule of thumb for handling graphics in desktop publishing applications EXCEPT  12._____

    A. using pie charts for showing parts of a whole
    B. showing data relationships with line plots
    C. using serif typefaces in graph labels
    D. using bar charts to shown quantities of a single item

13. The central liability-related ethical issue raised by new information technologies is generally considered to be  13._____

    A. whether software or other intellectual property may be copied for personal use
    B. the point at which it is justifiable to release software or services for consumption by others
    C. the conditions under which it is justifiable to invade the privacy of others
    D. whether individuals and organizations that create, produce, and sell systems are morally responsible for the consequences of their use

14. Which of the following personnel would be considered part of the development team in an MIS department?  14._____

    A. Control clerk         B. Maintenance programmer
    C. Education specialist      D. Data administrator

15. Which of the following is an object-oriented programming language that can deliver only the software functionality needed for a particular task, and which can run on any computer or operating system?  15._____

    A. Perl        B. C        C. Linux        D. Java

16. Which of the following is NOT typically an example of the inquiry/response type of telecommunications application?  16._____

    A. Point-of-sale system
    B. Airline reservation system
    C. Hospital information system
    D. Credit checking

17. Which of the following is an example of work-flow management?    17.____

    A. Financial officers at a firm use a computer program to calculate the rate of return for specific investments.

    B. A manager views a company's quarterly revenues from her own workstation without the need for printed matter.

    C. Loan officers at a bank enter application information into a central system so that the application can be evaluated by many people at once.

    D. Cashiers at a retail outlet scan the bar codes on items of merchandise to more quickly move customers through the checkout.

18. According to Simon's description, there are four stages in any decision-making process. Decision support systems are designed primarily to help monitor the _____ stage.    18.____

    A. implementation            B. design

    C. choice                  D. intelligence

19. A form of organization resembling a fishnet or network, in which authority is determined by knowledge and function, is a    19.____

    A. hierarchy              B. matrix

    C. heterarchy            D. homeostat

20. What is the term used to describe the approach to software development that combines data and procedures into a single item?    20.____

    A. Operational           B. Object-oriented

    C. Output controlled      D. Transactional

21. Which of the following is a computer language that is an application generator?    21.____

    A. SQL        B. Nomad        C. AMAPS        D. FOCUS

22. Approximately what percentage of an organization's software development budget will be expended on testing?    22.____

    A. 10-20        B. 15-35        C. 30-50        D. 55-75

23. The process embodied in an input-output device, which enables it to convert or code without memory a type of signal, motion, or sequence of characters into another, is known as    23.____

    A. telematics           B. polarity

    C. reification           D. transduction

24. Which of the following steps in the business systems planning (BSP) process is typically performed FIRST?    24.____

    A. Defining business processes

    B. Analyzing current systems support

    C. Defining information architecture

    D. Developing recommendations

25. What is the term for a networking technology that parcels information into 8-byte cells, allowing data to be transmitted between computers of different vendors at any speed?

    A. Indexed sequential access method (ISAM)
    B. Asynchronous transfer mode (ATM)
    C. Private branch exchange (PBX)
    D. Domestic export

25.____

---

# KEY (CORRECT ANSWERS)

| | | | |
|---|---|---|---|
| 1. | B | 11. | D |
| 2. | A | 12. | C |
| 3. | B | 13. | D |
| 4. | C | 14. | B |
| 5. | C | 15. | D |
| 6. | D | 16. | C |
| 7. | C | 17. | C |
| 8. | D | 18. | A |
| 9. | D | 19. | C |
| 10. | A | 20. | B |

| | |
|---|---|
| 21. | D |
| 22. | C |
| 23. | D |
| 24. | A |
| 25. | B |

---

# TEST 2

DIRECTIONS: Each question or incomplete statement is followed by several suggested answers or completions. Select the one that BEST answers the question or completes the statement. *PRINT THE LETTER OF THE CORRECT ANSWER IN THE SPACE AT THE RIGHT.*

1. *Intelligent agent* software is an appropriate tool for each of the following applications EXCEPT

    A. finding cheap airfares
    B. conducting data conferences
    C. scheduling appointments
    D. deleting junk e-mail

1.____

2. Which of the following is the general term for high-speed digital communications networks that are national or worldwide in scope and accessible by the general public?

    A. Wide-area networks (WANs)
    B. Internet
    C. World Wide Web
    D. Information superhighway

2.____

3. Which of the following types of organizations is LEAST likely to make use of a hierarchical database?

    A. Insurance companies
    B. Consultancies/service organizations
    C. Banks
    D. National retailers

3.____

4. A transmission rate of _____ per second falls within the normal range for a local-area network.

    A. 70 bits                 B. 100 kilobits
    C. 100 megabits       D. 3 gigabits

4.____

5. In the history of artificial intelligence, the effort to build a physical analog to the human brain has been referred to as the _____ approach.

    A. schematic           B. sequential
    C. neuronet            D. bottom-up

5.____

6. In an individual MIS, the most commonly-used technique for conducting operations research is _____ programming.

    A. productivity         B. statistical
    C. management       D. linear

6.____

7. Of the types of organizational change that are enabled by information technology, which tends to be the most common?

    A. Paradigm shift
    B. Automation
    C. Business reengineering
    D. Rationalization of procedures

7.____

8. Which of the following is offered the clearest protection under the Electronic Communications Privacy Act of 1986?   8.____

   A. Personal e-mail received from outside by the organization's system
   B. Interoffice fax transmissions
   C. Business-related phone calls received from outside by the organization's system
   D. Interoffice e-mail

9. Which of the following systems exists at the operational level of an organization?   9.____

   A. Transaction processing system (TPS)
   B. Executive support system (ESS)
   C. Office automation system (OAS)
   D. Management information system (MIS)

10. The representation of data as they appear to an application programmer or end user is described as a(n) _____ view.   10.____

    A. schematic          B. analogous
    C. logical            D. physical

11. Which of the computer hardware *generations* involved vacuum tube technology?   11.____

    A. First          B. Second          C. Third          D. Fourth

12. Which of the following is an example of the administrative message switching application of telecommunications technology?   12.____

    A. Inventory control
    B. Electronic mail
    C. Library systems
    D. International transfer of bank funds

13. Which of the following styles of systems development is most often used for information systems at the enterprise level?   13.____

    A. Prototyping          B. Outsourcing
    C. End-user development  D. Traditional life cycle

14. Which of the following is an element of the physical design of an information system?   14.____

    A. Manual procedures     B. Input descriptions
    C. Processing functions  D. Controls

15. Which of the following functions to connect dissimilar networks by providing the translation from one protocol to another?   15.____

    A. Gateway          B. Assembler          C. Gopher          D. Buffer

16. The primary memory of most microcomputers is measured in   16.____

    A. megabytes          B. gigabytes          C. kilobytes          D. bytes

17. _____ tools is a project management technique that structures and sequences tasks, and budgets the time, money, and technical resources required to complete these tasks.   17.____

    A. Internal integration   B. Formal control
    C. External integration   D. Formal planning

18. What is the term for the capacity of a communications channel as measured by the difference between the highest and lowest frequencies that can be transmitted by that channel?

    A. Transmissivity                B. Broadband
    C. Baud rate                     D. Bandwidth

18.\_\_\_\_

19. Which of the following are LEAST likely to be an input into a management information
system (MIS)?

    A. Design specifications         B. Simple models
    C. Summary transaction data    D. High-volume data

19.\_\_\_\_

20. Which of the following is a shared network service technology that packages data into
bundles for transmission but does not use error correction routines?

    A. Private branch exchange     B. Packet switching
    C. Internal integration          D. Frame relay

20.\_\_\_\_

21. A purpose of a file server in a network is to

    A. collect messages for batch transmission
    B. route communications
    C. store programs
    D. connect dissimilar networks

21.\_\_\_\_

22. _____ testing provides the final certification that a new system is ready to be used in a
production setting.

    A. Parallel                  B. Unit
    C. Acceptance              D. System

22.\_\_\_\_

23. The number of _____ is NOT an example of software metrics.

    A. payroll checks printed per hour
    B. known users who are dissatisfied with an application's performance
    C. transactions that can be processed in one business day
    D. known bugs per hundred lines of code

23.\_\_\_\_

24. What is the term for a set or rules that govern the manipulation of characters in a system?

    A. Synergy                 B. Entropy
    C. Aggregation             D. Calculus

24.\_\_\_\_

25. During the process of enterprise analysis, the results of a large managerial survey are
broken down into each of the following EXCEPT

    A. processes               B. goals
    C. data matrices            D. functions

25.\_\_\_\_

# KEY (CORRECT ANSWERS)

| | | | |
|---|---|---|---|
| 1. | B | 11. | A |
| 2. | D | 12. | B |
| 3. | B | 13. | D |
| 4. | C | 14. | A |
| 5. | D | 15. | A |
| 6. | D | 16. | C |
| 7. | B | 17. | D |
| 8. | A | 18. | D |
| 9. | A | 19. | A |
| 10. | C | 20. | D |

| | |
|---|---|
| 21. | C |
| 22. | C |
| 23. | B |
| 24. | D |
| 25. | B |

———

# RECORD KEEPING
# EXAMINATION SECTION
# TEST 1

DIRECTIONS: Each question or incomplete statement is followed by several suggested answers or completions. Select the one that BEST answers the question or completes the statement. *PRINT THE LETTER OF THE CORRECT ANSWER IN THE SPACE AT THE RIGHT.*

Questions 1-15.

DIRECTIONS: Questions 1 through 15 are to be answered on the basis of the following list of company names below. Arrange a file alphabetically, word-by-word, disregarding punctuation, conjunctions, and apostrophes. Then answer the questions.

A Bee C Reading Materials
ABCO Parts
A Better Course for Test Preparation
AAA Auto Parts Co.
A-Z Auto Parts, Inc.
Aabar Books
Abbey, Joanne
Boman-Sylvan Law Firm
BMW Autowerks
C Q Service Company
Chappell-Murray, Inc.
E&E Life Insurance
Emcrisco
Gigi Arts
Gordon, Jon & Associates
SOS Plumbing
Schmidt, J.B. Co.

1. Which of these files should appear FIRST?                          1.____

   A. ABCO Parts
   B. A Bee C Reading Materials
   C. A Better Course for Test Preparation
   D. AAA Auto Parts Co.

2. Which of these files should appear SECOND?                         2.____

   A. A-Z Auto Parts, Inc.
   B. A Bee C Reading Materials
   C. A Better Course for Test Preparation
   D. AAA Auto Parts Co.

3. Which of these files should appear THIRD?                          3.____

   A. ABCO Parts
   B. A Bee C Reading Materials
   C. Aabar Books
   D. AAA Auto Parts Co.

4. Which of these files should appear FOURTH?    4.\_\_\_\_

   A. Aabar Books
   B. ABCO Parts
   C. Abbey, Joanne
   D. AAA Auto Parts Co.

5. Which of these files should appear LAST?    5.\_\_\_\_

   A. Gordon, Jon & Associates
   B. Gigi Arts
   C. Schmidt, J.B. Co.
   D. SOS Plumbing

6. Which of these files should appear between A-Z Auto Parts, Inc. and Abbey, Joanne?    6.\_\_\_\_

   A. A Bee C Reading Materials
   B. AAA Auto Parts Co.
   C. ABCO Parts
   D. A Better Course for Test Preparation

7. Which of these files should appear between ABCO Parts and Aabar Books?    7.\_\_\_\_

   A. A Bee C Reading Materials
   B. Abbey, Joanne
   C. Aabar Books
   D. A-Z Auto Parts

8. Which of these files should appear between Abbey, Joanne and Boman-Sylvan Law Firm?    8.\_\_\_\_

   A. A Better Course for Test Preparation
   B. BMW Autowerks
   C. Chappell-Murray, Inc.
   D. Aabar Books

9. Which of these files should appear between Abbey, Joanne and C Q Service?    9.\_\_\_\_

   A. A-Z Auto Parts,Inc.      B. BMW Autowerks
   C. Choices A and B         D. Chappell-Murray, Inc.

10. Which of these files should appear between C Q Service Company and Emcrisco?    10.\_\_\_\_

   A. Chappell-Murray, Inc.     B. E&E Life Insurance
   C. Gigi Arts             D. Choices A and B

11. Which of these files should NOT appear between C Q Service Company and E&E Life Insurance?    11.\_\_\_\_

   A. Gordon, Jon & Associates
   B. Emcrisco
   C. Gigi Arts
   D. All of the above

12. Which of these files should appear between Chappell-Murray Inc., and Gigi Arts?      12.____

    A. CQ Service Inc. E&E Life Insurance, and Emcrisco
    B. Emcrisco, E&E Life Insurance, and Gordon, Jon & Associates
    C. E&E Life Insurance and Emcrisco
    D. Emcrisco and Gordon, Jon & Associates

13. Which of these files should appear between Gordon, Jon & Associates and SOS Plumb-      13.____
ing?

    A. Gigi Arts                B. Schmidt, J.B. Co.
    C. Choices A and B       D. None of the above

14. Each of the choices lists the four files in their proper alphabetical order except      14.____

    A. E&E Life Insurance; Gigi Arts; Gordon, Jon & Associates; SOS Plumbing
    B. E&E Life Insurance; Emcrisco; Gigi Arts; SOS Plumbing
    C. Emcrisco; Gordon, Jon & Associates; SOS Plumbing; Schmidt, J.B. Co.
    D. Emcrisco; Gigi Arts; Gordon, Jon & Associates; SOS Plumbing

15. Which of the choices lists the four files in their proper alphabetical order?      15.____

    A. Gigi Arts; Gordon, Jon & Associates; SOS Plumbing; Schmidt, J.B. Co.
    B. Gordon, Jon & Associates; Gigi Arts; Schmidt, J.B. Co.; SOS Plumbing
    C. Gordon, Jon & Associates; Gigi Arts; SOS Plumbing; Schmidt, J.B. Co.
    D. Gigi Arts; Gordon, Jon & Associates; Schmidt, J.B. Co.; SOS Plumbing

16. The alphabetical filing order of two businesses with identical names is determined by the      16.____

    A. length of time each business has been operating
    B. addresses of the businesses
    C. last name of the company president
    D. none of the above

17. In an alphabetical filing system, if a business name includes a number, it should be      17.____

    A. disregarded
    B. considered a number and placed at the end of an alphabetical section
    C. treated as though it were written in words and alphabetized accordingly
    D. considered a number and placed at the beginning of an alphabetical section

18. If a business name includes a contraction (such as *don't* or *it's*), how should that word be      18.____
treated in an alphabetical filing system?

    A. Divide the word into its separate parts and treat it as two words.
    B. Ignore the letters that come after the apostrophe.
    C. Ignore the word that contains the contraction.
    D. Ignore the apostrophe and consider all letters in the contraction.

19. In what order should the parts of an address be considered when using an alphabetical      19.____
filing system?

    A. City or town; state; street name; house or building number
    B. State; city or town; street name; house or building number
    C. House or building number; street name; city or town; state
    D. Street name; city or town; state

20. A business record should be cross-referenced when a(n)  20.___

    A. organization is known by an abbreviated name
    B. business has a name change because of a sale, incorporation, or other reason
    C. business is known by a *coined* or common name which differs from a dictionary spelling
    D. all of the above

21. A geographical filing system is MOST effective when  21.___

    A. location is more important than name
    B. many names or titles sound alike
    C. dealing with companies who have offices all over the world
    D. filing personal and business files

Questions 22-25.

DIRECTIONS:    Questions 22 through 25 are to be answered on the basis of the list of items below, which are to be filed geographically. Organize the items geographically and then answer the questions.
    1. University Press at Berkeley, U.S.
    2. Maria Sanchez, Mexico City, Mexico
    3. Great Expectations Ltd. in London, England
    4. Justice League, Cape Town, South Africa, Africa
    5. Crown Pearls Ltd. in London, England
    6. Joseph Prasad in London, England

22. Which of the following arrangements of the items is composed according to the policy of:  22.___
*Continent, Country, City, Firm or Individual Name?*

    A. 5, 3, 4, 6, 2, 1        B. 4, 5, 3, 6, 2, 1
    C. 1, 4, 5, 3, 6, 2        D. 4, 5, 3, 6, 1, 2

23. Which of the following files is arranged according to the policy of: *Continent, Country,*  23.___
*City, Firm or Individual Name?*

    A. South Africa. Africa. Cape Town. Justice League
    B. Mexico. Mexico City, Maria Sanchez
    C. North America. United States. Berkeley. University Press
    D. England. Europe. London. Prasad, Joseph

24. Which of the following arrangements of the items is composed according to the policy of:  24.___
*Country, City, Firm or Individual Name?*

    A. 5, 6, 3, 2, 4, 1        B. 1, 5, 6, 3, 2, 4
    C. 6, 5, 3, 2, 4, 1        D. 5, 3, 6, 2, 4, 1

25. Which of the following files is arranged according to a policy of: *Country, City, Firm or*  25.___
*Individual Name?*

    A. England. London. Crown Pearls Ltd.
    B. North America. United States. Berkeley. University Press
    C. Africa. Cape Town. Justice League
    D. Mexico City. Mexico. Maria Sanchez

26. Under which of the following circumstances would a phonetic filing system be MOST effective?  26.____

    A. When the person in charge of filing can't spell very well
    B. With large files with names that sound alike
    C. With large files with names that are spelled alike
    D. All of the above

Questions 27-29.

DIRECTIONS: Questions 27 through 29 are to be answered on the basis of the following list of numerical files.

    1. 391-023-100
    2. 361-132-170
    3. 385-732-200
    4. 381-432-150
    5. 391-632-387
    6. 361-423-303
    7. 391-123-271

27. Which of the following arrangements of the files follows a consecutive-digit system?  27.____

    A. 2, 3, 4, 1               B. 1, 5, 7, 3
    C. 2, 4, 3, 1               D. 3, 1, 5, 7

28. Which of the following arrangements follows a terminal-digit system?  28.____

    A. 1, 7, 2, 4, 3           B. 2, 1, 4, 5, 7
    C. 7, 6, 5, 4, 3           D. 1, 4, 2, 3, 7

29. Which of the following lists follows a middle-digit system?  29.____

    A. 1, 7, 2, 6, 4, 5, 3     B. 1, 2, 7, 4, 6, 5, 3
    C. 7, 2, 1, 3, 5, 6, 4     D. 7, 1, 2, 4, 6, 5, 3

Questions 30-31.

DIRECTIONS: Questions 30 and 31 are to be answered on the basis of the following information.
    1. Reconfirm Laura Bates appointment with James Caldecort on December 12 at 9:30 A.M.
    2. Laurence Kinder contact Julia Lucas on August 3 and set up a meeting for week of September 23 at 4 P.M.
    3. John Lutz contact Larry Waverly on August 3 and set up appointment for September 23 at 9:30 A.M.
    4. Call for tickets for Gerry Stanton August 21 for New Jersey on September 23, flight 143 at 4:43 P.M.

30. A chronological file for the above information would be                                      30.____

    A. 4, 3, 2, 1                         B. 3, 2, 4, 1
    C. 4, 2, 3, 1                         D. 3, 1, 2, 4

31. Using the above information, a chronological file for the date of September 23 would be      31.____

    A. 2, 3, 4         B. 3, 1, 4         C. 3, 2, 4         D. 4, 3, 2

Questions 32-34.

DIRECTIONS:   Questions 32 through 34 are to be answered on the basis of the following information.

1. Call Roger Epstein, Ashoke Naipaul, Jon Anderson, and Sarah Washington on April 19 at 1:00 P.M. to set up meeting with Alika D'Ornay for June 6 in New York.
2. Call Martin Ames before noon on April 19 to confirm afternoon meeting with Bob Greenwood on April 20th
3. Set up meeting room at noon for 2:30 P.M. meeting on April 19th;
4. Ashley Stanton contact Bob Greenwood at 9:00 A.M. on April 20 and set up meeting for June 6 at 8:30 A.M.
5. Carol Guiland contact Shelby Van Ness during afternoon of April 20 and set up meeting for June 6 at 10:00 A.M.
6. Call airline and reserve tickets on June 6 for Roger Epstein trip *to* Denver on July 8
7. Meeting at 2:30 P.M. on April 19th

32. A chronological file for all of the above information would be                                32.____

    A. 2, 1, 3, 7, 5, 4, 6               B. 3, 7, 2, 1, 4, 5, 6
    C. 3, 7, 1, 2, 5, 4, 6               D. 2, 3, 1, 7, 4, 5, 6

33. A chronological file for the date of April 19th would be                                     33.____

    A. 2, 3, 7, 1                      B. 2, 3, 1, 7
    C. 7, 1, 3, 2                      D. 3, 7, 1, 2

34. Add the following information to the file, and then create a chronological file for April 20th:   34.____
    8. April 20: 3:00 P.M. meeting between Bob Greenwood and Martin Ames.

    A. 4, 5, 8         B. 4, 8, 5         C. 8, 5, 4         D. 5, 4, 8

35. The PRIMARY advantage of computer records filing over a manual system is                     35.____

    A. speed of retrieval                 B. accuracy
    C. cost                           D. potential file loss

# KEY (CORRECT ANSWERS)

| | | | |
|---|---|---|---|
| 1. | B | 16. | B |
| 2. | C | 17. | C |
| 3. | D | 18. | D |
| 4. | A | 19. | A |
| 5. | D | 20. | D |
| 6. | C | 21. | A |
| 7. | B | 22. | B |
| 8. | B | 23. | C |
| 9. | C | 24. | D |
| 10. | D | 25. | A |
| 11. | D | 26. | B |
| 12. | C | 27. | C |
| 13. | B | 28. | D |
| 14. | C | 29. | A |
| 15. | D | 30. | B |

| | |
|---|---|
| 31. | C |
| 32. | D |
| 33. | B |
| 34. | A |
| 35. | A |

# NAME AND NUMBER CHECKING

## EXAMINATION SECTION
## TEST 1

DIRECTIONS: This test is designed to measure your speed and accuracy. You are urged to work both quickly and accurately and to do correctly as many lists as you can in the time allowed. The test consists of lists of pairs of names and numbers. Count the number of IDENTICAL pairs in each list. Then, select the correct number, 1, 2, 3, 4, or 5, and indicate your choice by circling the corresponding number on your answer paper, Two sample questions are presented for your guidance, together with the correct solutions.

### SAMPLE QUESTIONS

|  |  | CIRCLE CORRECT ANSWER |
|---|---|---|
| SAMPLE LIST A | | |
| Adelphi College | - Adelphia College | 1  2  3  4  5 |
| Braxton Corp. | - Braxeton Corp. | |
| Wassaic State School | - Wassaic State School | |
| Central Islip State Hospital | - Central Isllip State | |
| Greenwich House | - Greenwich House | |

*NOTE that there are only two correct pairs - Wassaic State School and Greenwich House. Therefore, the CORRECT answer is 2.*

| SAMPLE LIST B | | |
|---|---|---|
| 78453694 | - 78453684 | 1  2  3  4  5 |
| 784530 | - 784530 | |
| 533 | - 534 | |
| 67845 | - 67845 | |
| 2368745 | - 2368755 | |

*NOTE that there are only two correct pairs - 784530 and 67845. Therefore, the CORRECT answer is 2.*

LIST 1

| 98654327 | - 98654327 | 1  2  3  4  5 |
|---|---|---|
| 74932564 | - 74922564 | |
| 61438652 | - 61438652 | |
| 01297653 | - 01287653 | |
| 1865439765 | - 1865439765 | |

LIST 2

| 478362 | - 478363 | 1  2  3  4  5 |
|---|---|---|
| 278354792 | - 278354772 | |
| 9327 | - 9327 | |
| 297384625 | - 27384625 | |
| 6428156 | - 6428158 | |

LIST 3

| Abbey House | - Abbey House | 1 | 2 | 3 | 4 | 5 |
| Actors' Fund Home | - Actor's Fund Home | | | | | |
| Adrian Memorial | - Adrian Memorial | | | | | |
| A. Clayton Powell Home | - Clayton Powell House | | | | | |
| Abott E. Kittredge Club | - Abbott E. Kitteredge Club | | | | | |

LIST 4

| 3682 | - 3692 | 1 | 2 | 3 | 4 | 5 |
| 21937453829 | - 31937453829 | | | | | |
| 723 | - 733 | | | | | |
| 2763920 | - 2763920 | | | | | |
| 47293 | - 47293 | | | | | |

LIST 5

| Adra House | - Adra House | 1 | 2 | 3 | 4 | 5 |
| Adolescents' Court | - Adolescents' Court | | | | | |
| Cliff Villa | - Cliff Villa | | | | | |
| Clark Neighborhood House | - Clark Neighborhood House | | | | | |
| Alma Mathews House | - Alma Mathews House | | | | | |

LIST 6

| 28734291 | - 28734271 | 1 | 2 | 3 | 4 | 5 |
| 63810263849 | - 63810263846 | | | | | |
| 26831027 | - 26831027 | | | | | |
| 368291 | - 368291 | | | | | |
| 7238102637 | - 7238102637 | | | | | |

LIST 7

| Albion State T.S. | - Albion State T.C. | 1 | 2 | 3 | 4 | 5 |
| Clara de Hirsch Home | - Clara De Hirsch Home | | | | | |
| Alice Carrington Royce | - Alice Carington Royce | | | | | |
| Alice Chopin Nursery | - Alice Chapin Nursery | | | | | |
| Lighthouse Eye Clinic | - Lighthouse Eye Clinic | | | | | |

LIST 8

| 327 | - 329 | 1 | 2 | 3 | 4 | 5 |
| 712438291026 | - 712438291026 | | | | | |
| 2753829142 | - 275382942 | | | | | |
| 826287 | - 826289 | | | | | |
| 26435162839 | - 26435162839 | | | | | |

LIST 9

| Letchworth Village | - Letchworth Village | 1 | 2 | 3 | 4 | 5 |
| A.A.A.E. Inc. | - A.A.A.E. Inc. | | | | | |
| Clear Pool Camp | - Clear Pool Camp | | | | | |
| A.M.M.L.A. Inc. | - A.M.M.L.A. Inc. | | | | | |
| J.G. Harbard | - J.G. Harbord | | | | | |

CIRCLE
CORRECT ANSWER

LIST 10

| | | 1 | 2 | 3 | 4 | 5 |
|---|---|---|---|---|---|---|
| 8254 | - 8256 | | | | | |
| 2641526 | - 2641526 | | | | | |
| 4126389012 | - 4126389102 | | | | | |
| 725 | - 725 | | | | | |
| 76253917287 | - 76253917287 | | | | | |

LIST 11

| | | 1 | 2 | 3 | 4 | 5 |
|---|---|---|---|---|---|---|
| Attica State Prison | - Attica State Prison | | | | | |
| Nellie Murrah | - Nellie Murrah | | | | | |
| Club Marshall | - Club Marshal | | | | | |
| Assissium Casea-Maria | - Assissium Casa-Maria | | | | | |
| The Homestead | - The Homestead | | | | | |

LIST 12

| | | 1 | 2 | 3 | 4 | 5 |
|---|---|---|---|---|---|---|
| 2691 | - 2691 | | | | | |
| 623819253627 | - 623819253629 | | | | | |
| 28637 | - 28937 | | | | | |
| 278392736 | - 278392736 | | | | | |
| 52739 | - 52739 | | | | | |

LIST 13

| | | 1 | 2 | 3 | 4 | 5 |
|---|---|---|---|---|---|---|
| A.I.C.P. Boys Camp | - A.I.C.P. Boy's Camp | | | | | |
| Einar Chrystie | - Einar Christyie | | | | | |
| Astoria Center | - Astoria Center | | | | | |
| G. Frederick Brown | - G. Federick Browne | | | | | |
| Vacation Service | - Vacation Services | | | | | |

LIST 14

| | | 1 | 2 | 3 | 4 | 5 |
|---|---|---|---|---|---|---|
| 728352689 | - 728352688 | | | | | |
| 643728 | - 643728 | | | | | |
| 37829176 | - 37827196 | | | | | |
| 8425367 | - 8425369 | | | | | |
| 65382018 | - 65382018 | | | | | |

LIST 15

| | | 1 | 2 | 3 | 4 | 5 |
|---|---|---|---|---|---|---|
| E.S. Streim | - E.S. Strim | | | | | |
| Charles E. Higgins | - Charles E. Higgins | | | | | |
| Baluvelt, N.Y. | - Blauwelt, N.Y. | | | | | |
| Roberta Magdalen | - Roberto Magdalen | | | | | |
| Ballard School | - Ballard School | | | | | |

LIST 16

| | | 1 | 2 | 3 | 4 | 5 |
|---|---|---|---|---|---|---|
| 7382 | - 7392 | | | | | |
| 281374538299 | - 291374538299 | | | | | |
| 623 | - 633 | | | | | |
| 6273730 | - 6273730 | | | | | |
| 63392 | - 63392 | | | | | |

CIECLE
CORRECT ANSWER

## LIST 17
| | | | | | | | |
|---|---|---|---|---|---|---|---|
| Orrin Otis | - Orrin Otis | 1 | 2 | 3 | 4 | 5 |
| Barat Settlement | - Barat Settlemen | | | | | |
| Emmanuel House | - Emmanuel House | | | | | |
| William T. McCreery | - William T. McCreery | | | | | |
| Seamen's Home | - Seaman's Home | | | | | |

## LIST 18
| | | | | | | | |
|---|---|---|---|---|---|---|---|
| 72824391 | - 72834371 | 1 | 2 | 3 | 4 | 5 |
| 3729106237 | - 37291106237 | | | | | |
| 82620163849 | - 82620163846 | | | | | |
| 37638921 | - 37638921 | | | | | |
| 82631027 | - 82631027 | | | | | |

## LIST 19
| | | | | | | | |
|---|---|---|---|---|---|---|---|
| Commonwealth Fund | - Commonwealth Fund | 1 | 2 | 3 | 4 | 5 |
| Anne Johnsen | - Anne Johnson | | | | | |
| Bide-a-Wee Home | - Bide-a-Wee Home | | | | | |
| Riverdale-on-Hudson | - Riverdal-on-Hudson | | | | | |
| Bialystoker Home | - Bailystoker Home | | | | | |

## LIST 20
| | | | | | | | |
|---|---|---|---|---|---|---|---|
| 9271 | - 9271 | 1 | 2 | 3 | 4 | 5 |
| 392918352627 | - 392018852629 | | | | | |
| 72637 | - 72637 | | | | | |
| 927392736 | - 927392736 | | | | | |
| 92739 | - 92739 | | | | | |

## LIST 21
| | | | | | | | |
|---|---|---|---|---|---|---|---|
| Charles M. Stump | - Charles M. Stump | 1 | 2 | 3 | 4 | 5 |
| Bourne Workshop | - Buorne Workshop | | | | | |
| B'nai Bi'rith | - B'nai Brith | | | | | |
| Poppenhuesen Institute | - Poppenheusen Institute | | | | | |
| Consular Service | - Consular Service | | | | | |

## LIST 22
| | | | | | | | |
|---|---|---|---|---|---|---|---|
| 927352689 | - 927352688 | 1 | 2 | 3 | 4 | 5 |
| 647382 | - 648382 | | | | | |
| 93729176 | - 93727196 | | | | | |
| 649536718 | - 649536718 | | | | | |
| 5835367 | - 5835369 | | | | | |

## LIST 23
| | | | | | | | |
|---|---|---|---|---|---|---|---|
| L.S. Bestend | - L.S. Bestent | 1 | 2 | 3 | 4 | 5 |
| Hirsch Mfg. Co. | - Hircsh Mfg. Co. | | | | | |
| F.H. Storrs | - F.P. Storrs | | | | | |
| Camp Wassaic | - Camp Wassaic | | | | | |
| George Ballingham | - George Ballingham | | | | | |

LIST 24

| | | |
|---|---|---|
| 372846392048 | - 372846392048 | 1 2 3 4 5 |
| 334 | - 334 | |
| 7283524678 | - 7283524678 | |
| 7283 | - 7283 | |
| 7283629372 | - 7283629372 | |

LIST 25

| | | |
|---|---|---|
| Dr. Stiles Company | - Dr. Stills Company | 1 2 3 4 5 |
| Frances Hunsdon | - Frances Hunsdon | |
| Northrop Barrert | - Nothrup Barrent | |
| J. D. Brunjes | - J. D. Brunjes | |
| Theo. Claudel & Co. | - Theo. Claudel co. | |

# KEY (CORRECT ANSWERS)

| | | | | |
|---|---|---|---|---|
| 1. | 3 | | 11. | 3 |
| 2. | 1 | | 12. | 3 |
| 3. | 2 | | 13. | 1 |
| 4. | 2 | | 14. | 2 |
| 5. | 5 | | 15. | 2 |
| | | | | |
| 6. | 3 | | 16. | 2 |
| 7. | 1 | | 17. | 3 |
| 8. | 2 | | 18. | 2 |
| 9. | 4 | | 19. | 2 |
| 10. | 3 | | 20. | 4 |

| | |
|---|---|
| 21. | 2 |
| 22. | 1 |
| 23. | 2 |
| 24. | 5 |
| 25. | 2 |

# TEST 2

DIRECTIONS: This test is designed to measure your speed and accuracy. You are urged to work both quickly and accurately and to do correctly as many lists as you can in the time allowed. The test consists of lists of pairs of names and numbers. Count the number of IDENTICAL pairs in each list. Then, select the correct number, 1, 2, 3, 4, or 5, and indicate your choice by circling the corresponding number on your answer paper, Two sample questions are presented for your guidance, together with the correct solutions.

LIST 1

| | | |
|---|---|---|
| 82728 | - 82738 | CIRCLE |
| 82736292637 | - 82736292639 | CORRECT ANSWER |
| 728 | - 738 | 1 2 3 4 5 |
| 83926192527 | - 83726192529 | |
| 82736272 | - 82736272 | |

LIST 2

| | | |
|---|---|---|
| L. Pietri | - L. Pietri | |
| Mathewson, L.F. | - Mathewson, L.F. | |
| Funk & Wagnall | - Funk &. Wagnalls | 1 2 3 4 5 |
| Shimizu, Sojio | - Shimizu, Sojio | |
| Filing Equipment Bureau | - Filing Equipment Buraeu | |

LIST 3

| | | |
|---|---|---|
| 63801829374 | - 63801839474 | |
| 283577657 | - 283577657 | |
| 65689 | - 65689 | 1 2 3 4 5 |
| 3457892026 | - 3547893026 | |
| 2779 | - 2778 | |

LIST 4

| | | |
|---|---|---|
| August Caille | - August Caille | |
| The Well-Fare Service | - The Wel-Fare Service | |
| K.L.M. Process Co. | - R.L.M. Process Co. | 1 2 3 4 5 |
| Merrill Littell | - Merrill Littell | |
| Dodd & Sons | - Dodd & Son | |

LIST 5

| | | |
|---|---|---|
| 998745732 | - 998745733 | |
| 723 | - 723 | |
| 463849102983 | - 463849102983 | 1 2 3 4 5 |
| 8570 | - 8570 | |
| 279012 | - 279012 | |

LIST 6

| | | |
|---|---|---|
| M. A. Wender | - M.A. Winder | |
| Minneapolis Supply Co. | - Minneapolis Supply Co. | |
| Beverly Hills Corp | - Beverley Hills Corp. | 1 2 3 4 5 |
| Trafalgar Square | - Trafalgar Square | |
| Phifer, D.T. | - Phiefer, D.T. | |

LIST 7

| 7834629 | - 7834629 | 1 2 3 4 5 |
| 3549806746 | - 3549806746 | |
| 97802564 | - 97892564 | |
| 689246 | - 688246 | |
| 2578024683 | - 2578024683 | |

LIST 8

| Scadrons' | - Scadrons' | 1 2 3 4 5 |
| Gensen & Bro. | - Genson & Bro. | |
| Firestone Co. | - Firestone Co. | |
| H.L. Eklund · | - H.L. Eklund | |
| Oleomargarine Co. | - Oleomargarine Co. | |

LIST 9

| 782039485618 | - 782039485618 | 1 2 3 4 5 |
| 53829172639 | - 63829172639 | |
| 892 | - 892 | |
| 82937482 | - 829374820 | |
| 52937456 | - 53937456 | |

LIST 10

| First Nat'l Bank | - First Nat'l Bank | 1 2 3 4 5 |
| Sedgwick Machine Works | - Sedgewick Machine Works | |
| Hectographia Co. | - Hectographia Corp. | |
| Levet Bros. | - Levet Bros. | |
| Multistamp Co.,Inc. | - Multistamp Co.,Inc. | |

LIST 11

| 7293 | - 7293 | 1 2 3 4 5 |
| 6382910293 | - 6382910292 | |
| 981928374012 | - 981928374912 | |
| 58293 | - 58393 | |
| 18203649271 | - 283019283745 | |

LIST 12

| Lowrey Lb'r Co. | - Lowrey Lb'r Co. | 1 2 3 4 5 |
| Fidelity Service | - Fidelity Service | |
| Reumann, J.A. | - Reumann, J.A. | |
| Duophoto Ltd. | - Duophotos Ltd. | |
| John Jarratt | - John Jaratt | |

LIST 13

| 6820384 | - 6820384 | 1 2 3 4 5 |
| 383019283745 | - 383019283745 | |
| 63927102 | - 63928102 | |
| 91029354829 | - 91029354829 | |
| 58291728 | - 58291728 | |

LIST 14

| | | |
|---|---|---|
| Standard Press Co. | - Standard Press Co. | 1  2  3  4  5 |
| Reliant Mf'g. Co. | - Relant Mf'g Co. | |
| M.C. Lynn | - M.C. Lynn | |
| J. Fredericks Company | - G. Fredericks Company | |
| Wandermann, B.S. | - Wanderman, B.S. | |

LIST 15

| | | |
|---|---|---|
| 4283910293 | - 4283010203 | 1  2  3  4  5 |
| 992018273648 | - 992018273848 | |
| 620 | - 629 | |
| 752937273 | - 752937373 | |
| 5392 | - 5392 | |

LIST 16

| | | |
|---|---|---|
| Waldorf Hotel | - Waldorf Hotel | 1  2  3  4  5 |
| Aaron Machinery Co. | - Aaron Machinery Co. | |
| Caroline Ann Locke | - Caroline Anne Locke | |
| McCabe Mfg. Co. | - McCabe Mfg. Co. | |
| R.L. Landres | - R.L. Landers | |

LIST 17

| | | |
|---|---|---|
| 68391028364 | - 68391028394 | 1  2  3  4  5 |
| 68293 | - 68293 | |
| 739201 | - 739201 | |
| 72839201 | - 72839211 | |
| 739917 | - 739719 | |

LIST 18

| | | |
|---|---|---|
| Balsam M.M. | - Balsamm, M.M. | 1  2  3  4  5 |
| Steinway & Co. | - Stienway & M. Co. | |
| Eugene Elliott | - Eugene A. Elliott | |
| Leonard Loan Co. | - Leonard Loan Co. | |
| Frederick Morgan | - Frederick Morgen | |

LIST 19

| | | |
|---|---|---|
| 8929 | - 9820 | 1  2  3  4  5 |
| 392836472829 | - 392836472829 | |
| 462 | - 462 2039271 | |
| 827 | - 2039276837 | |
| 53829 | - 54829 | |

LIST 20

| | | |
|---|---|---|
| Danielson's Hofbrau | - Danielson's Hafbrau | 1  2  3  4  5 |
| Edward A. Truarme | - Edward A. Truame | |
| Insulite Co. | - Insulite Co. | |
| Reisler Shoe Corp, | - Rielser Shoe Corp. | |
| L.L. Thompson | - L.L. Thompson | |

LIST 21

| | | |
|---|---|---|
| 92839102837 | - 92839102837 | 1  2  3  4  5 |
| 58891028 | - 58891028 | |
| 7291728 | - 7291928 | |
| 272839102839 | - 272839102839 | |
| 428192 | - 428102 | |

LIST 22

| | | |
|---|---|---|
| K.L. Veiller | - K.L. Veiller | 1  2  3  4  5 |
| Webster, Roy | - Webster, Ray | |
| Drasner Spring Co. | - Drasner Spring Co. | |
| Edward J. Cravenport | - Edward J. Cravanport | |
| Harold Field | - Harold A. Field | |

LIST 23

| | | |
|---|---|---|
| 2293 | - 2293 | 1  2  3  4  5 |
| 4283910293 | - 5382910292 | |
| 871928374012 | - 871928374912 | |
| 68293 | - 68393 | |
| 8120364927 | - 81293649271 | |

LIST 24

| | | |
|---|---|---|
| Tappe, Inc | - Tappe, Inc. | 1  2  3  4  5 |
| A.M. Wentingworth | - A.M. Wentinworth | |
| Scott A. Elliott | - Scott A. Elliott | |
| Echeverria Corp. | - Echeverria Corp. | |
| Bradford Victor Company | - Bradford Victer Company | |

LIST 25

| | | |
|---|---|---|
| 4820384 | - 4820384 | 1  2  3  4  5 |
| 393019283745 | - 283919283745 | |
| 63927102 | - 63927102 | |
| 91029354829 | - 91029354829 | |
| 48291728 | - 48291728 | |

# KEY (CORRECT ANSWERS)

| | | | | |
|---|---|---|---|---|
| 1. | 1 | | 11. | 1 |
| 2. | 3 | | 12. | 3 |
| 3. | 2 | | 13. | 4 |
| 4. | 2 | | 14. | 2 |
| 5. | 4 | | 15. | 1 |
| 6. | 2 | | 16. | 3 |
| 7. | 3 | | 17. | 2 |
| 8. | 4 | | 18. | 1 |
| 9. | 2 | | 19. | 1 |
| 10. | 3 | | 20. | 2 |

| | |
|---|---|
| 21. | 3 |
| 22. | 2 |
| 23. | 1 |
| 24. | 2 |
| 25. | 4 |

# READING COMPREHENSION
## UNDERSTANDING AND INTERPRETING WRITTEN MATERIAL

# EXAMINATION SECTION
## TEST 1

DIRECTIONS:    Each question or incomplete statement is followed by several suggested answers or completions. Select the one that BEST answers the question or completes the statement. *PRINT THE LETTER OF THE CORRECT ANSWER IN THE SPACE AT THE RIGHT.*

Questions 1-7.

DIRECTIONS:    Questions 1 through 7 are to be answered SOLELY on the basis of the following passage.

The first step in establishing a programming development schedule is to rate the programs to be developed or to be maintained on the basis of complexity, size, and input-output complexity. The most experienced programmer should rate the program complexity based on the system flow chart. The same person should do all of the rating so that all programs are rated in the same manner. If possible, the same person who rates the complexity should estimate the program size based on the number of pages of coding. This rating can easily be checked, after coding has been completed, against the number of pages of coding actually produced. If there is consistent error in the estimates for program size, all future estimates should be corrected for this error or the estimating method reviewed.

The input-output rating is a mechanical count of the number of input and output units or tapes which the program uses. The objective is to measure the number of distinct files which the program must control.

After the ratings have been completed, the man-days required for each of the tasks can be calculated. Good judgment or, if available, a table of past experience is used to translate the ratings into man-days, the units in which the schedule is expressed. The calculations should keep the values for each task completely separate so that a later evaluation can be made by program, programmer, and function.

After the values have been calculated, it is a simple matter to establish a development schedule. This can be a simple bar chart which assigns work to specific programmers, a complex computer program using the *PERT* technique of critical path scheduling, or other useful type of document.

1.   The rating and estimating of the programs should be performed by                              1.____

    A.   the person who will do the programming
    B.   a programmer trainee
    C.   the most experienced programmer
    D.   the operations supervisor

2. The measurement used to express the programming schedule is the number of 2.____

    A. distinct files controlled by the programmer
    B. man-days
    C. pages of coding
    D. programmers

3. A mechanical count of the number of input and output units or tapes should be considered as a(n) 3.____

    A. input-output rating
    B. measure of the number of man-days required
    C. rating of complexity
    D. estimate of the number of pages of coding

4. Programming development scheduling methods are for 4.____

    A. new programs only
    B. programs to be developed and maintained
    C. large and complicated programs only
    D. maintenance programs only

5. If there is a consistent error in the estimates for program size, all estimates should be 5.____

    A. adjusted for future programs
    B. eliminated for all programs
    C. replaced by rating of complexity
    D. replaced by input-output rating

6. It is intimated that 6.____

    A. the calculations should keep the valuations for each task completely separated
    B. it is a simple matter to establish a development schedule
    C. the man-days required for each of the tasks can be calculated
    D. a later evaluation will be made

7. Complexity of programs can be checked 7.____

    A. before coding has been completed
    B. after future estimates have been corrected for error
    C. as a first step in establishing a complex computer program
    D. with reference to the number of pages of coding produced

Questions 8-13.

DIRECTIONS: Questions 8 through 13 are to be answered SOLELY on the basis of the following passage.

    The purposes of program testing are to determine that the program has been coded correctly, that the coding matches the logical design, and that the logical design matches the basic requirements of the job as set down in the specifications. Program errors fall into the following categories: errors in logic, clerical errors, misidentification of the computer components' functions, misinterpretation of the requirements of the job, and system analysis errors.

The number of errors in a program will average one for each 125 instructions, assuming that the programmer has been reasonably careful in his coding system. The number of permutations and combinations of conditions in a program may reach into the billions before each possibility has been thoroughly checked out. It is, therefore, a practical impossibility to check out each and every possible combination of conditions—the effort would take years, even in the simplest program. As a result, it is quite possible for errors to remain latent for a number of years, suddenly appearing when a particular combination is reached which had not previously occurred.

Latent program errors will remain in operating programs, and their occurrence should be minimized by complete and thorough testing. The fact that the program is operative and reaches end-of-job satisfactorily does not mean that all of the exception conditions and their permutations and combinations have been tested. Quite the contrary, many programs reach end-of-job after very few tests, since the *straight-line* part of the program is often simplest. However, the exceptions programmed to deal with a minimal percentage of the input account for a large percentage of the instructions. It is, therefore, quite possible to reach the end-of-job halt with only 10% of the program checked out.

8.  One of the MAIN points of this passage is that                                    8.____

    A.  it is impossible to do a good job of programming
    B.  reaching end-of-job means only 10% of the program is checked out
    C.  standard testing procedures should require testing of every possible combination
        of conditions
    D.  elimination of all errors can never be assured, but the occurrence of errors can be
        minimized by thorough testing

9.  Latent program errors GENERALLY                                                    9.____

    A.  evade detection for some time
    B.  are detected in the last test run
    C.  test the number of permutations and combinations in a program
    D.  allow the program to go to end-of-job

10. Which one of the following statements pertaining to errors in a program is CORRECT?   10.____

    A.  If the program has run to a normal completion, then all program errors have been
        eliminated.
    B.  Program errors, if not caught in testing, will surely be detected in the first hundred
        runs of the program.
    C.  It is practically impossible to verify that the typical program is free of errors.
    D.  A program that is coded correctly is free of errors.

11. Among other things, program testing is designed to                                 11.____

    A.  assure that the documentation is correct
    B.  assure that the coding is correct
    C.  determine the program running time
    D.  measure programmer's performance

12. The difficulty in detecting errors in programs is due to    12.____

    A. the extremely large number of conditions that exist in a program
    B. poor analysis of work errors
    C. very sophisticated and clever programming
    D. reaching the end-of-job halt with only 10% of the program checked out

13. If the program being tested finally reaches the end-of-job halt, it means that    13.____

    A. one path through the program has been successfully tested
    B. less than 10% of the program has been tested
    C. the program has been coded correctly
    D. the logical design is correct

Questions 14-20.

DIRECTIONS:   Questions 14 through 20 are to be answered SOLELY on the basis of the following passage.

    Systems analysis represents a major link in the chain of translations from the problem to its machine solution. After the problem and its requirements for solution have been stated in clear terms, the systems analyst defines the broad outlines of the machine solution. He must know the overall capabilities of the equipment, and he must be familiar with the application. The ultimate output of the analysis is a detailed job specification containing all the tools necessary to produce a series of computer programs. The purpose of the specifications is to document and describe the system by defining the problem and the proposed solution, explain system outputs and functions, state system requirements for programmers, and to avoid misunderstandings among involved departments. The specification serves as a link between the analysis of the problem and the next function, programming. Systems analysis relies on creativity rather than rote analysis to develop effective computer systems. But this creativity must be channeled and documented effectively if lasting value is to be obtained.

14. According to the above paragraph, the systems analyst MUST be familiar with    14.____

    A. programming and the machine solution
    B. the machine solution and the next function
    C. the application and programming
    D. the application and the equipment capabilities

15. According to the above paragraph, the time that systems analysis MUST be performed is    15.____

    A. *after* the problem analysis
    B. *after* programming
    C. *before* problem definition
    D. *before* problem analysis

16. According to the above paragraph, the MAIN task performed by the systems analyst is to    16.____

    A. write the program
    B. analyze the problem
    C. define the overall capacities of the equipment
    D. define the machine solution of the problem

17. According to the above paragraph, the document produced by the systems analyst as his main output does NOT normally include 17.____

    A. an explanation of system outputs
    B. system requirements for programmers
    C. a statement of the problem
    D. performance standards

18. According to the above paragraph, the systems analysis function is 18.____

    A. relatively straightforward, requiring little creative effort
    B. extremely complex, making standard procedures impossible
    C. primarily a rote memory procedure
    D. a creative effort

19. According to the above paragraph, the specification 19.____

    A. is a major link in the sequence from problem to machine solution
    B. states the problem and its requirements for solution
    C. is chiefly concerned with the overall capabilities of the equipment
    D. represents the ultimate product of systems analysis

20. According to the above paragraph, the sequential function after the analysis of the program is 20.____

    A. documentation          B. application
    C. definition             D. programming

Questions 21-25.

DIRECTIONS: Questions 21 through 25 are to be answered SOLELY on the basis of the following passage.

Currently, memory represents one of the main limitations on computer performance and, as a result, is one of the areas where technological improvements will prove most fruitful.

Historically, the main problem of computer memories has been a very unfavorable cost-to-speed ratio. Memory devices which have great speed cost disproportionately more than those with less speed. This problem has forced computer designers to use minimum amounts of rapid access memory and to rely mainly on slower, large capacity storage. This practice has resulted in a *memory tree,* where a hierarchy of memory devices provides various increments of storage at different costs and speeds for various purposes.

To achieve better speed/cost ratios, designers are increasingly turning to memory media other than the traditional ferrite cores. These cores now account for over 90% of the memory market. Plated wire and semiconductors are the media most likely to supplant ferrite cores. Semiconductors are expected to rapidly displace cores, starting with higher speed memories. Their costs are dropping sharply and are expected to drop as much as five-fold by the middle of this decade, while their speeds are at least doubling.

Despite the increasing use of competing technologies, ferrite cores will probably still dominate the extended random access storage area. Since the largest increment of storage is associated with ferrite core memory devices, their share of the internal memory market was well over 50% by 1980. The only factor militating against this is the possibility that the largest manufacturers of computers may abandon the extended internal storage concept.

Memory developments likely to happen later in this decade include the progressive replacement of magnetic drums by magnetic disks. The latter were themselves displaced near the end of the seventies by electro optical units, followed by magnetic bubble storage. It also may prove possible to show the feasibility of associative processors. Under this concept, which is still experimental, data access would be considerably speeded through use of Contents-Addressable-Memories (CAM).

21. According to the above passage, a hierarchy of memory devices which provides various increments of storage at different costs and speeds has been used by designers because    21.____

    A. one of the larger manufacturers of computers might abandon the extended internal storage concept
    B. of the very unfavorable cost-to-speed ratio of computer memories
    C. magnetic disks have progressively replaced magnetic drums in the mid-seventies
    D. data access is expected to be appreciably speeded up through the use of Content-Addressable-Memories

22. According to the above passage, which of the following memory developments is MOST likely to have occurred by 1980?    22.____

    A. Designers will turn to memories other than core for 90% of their needs.
    B. Cores and semiconductors will largely replace plated wire memories.
    C. Cores and semiconductors will largely be replaced by electro optical and magnetic bubble storage.
    D. Ferrite core will continue to dominate the internal memory market.

23. According to the above passage, the speed/cost ratio for semiconductors is    23.____

    A. becoming more favorable
    B. the same as the speed/cost ratio for plated wire
    C. remaining constant
    D. less favorable than the speed/cost ratio for ferrite core

24. According to the information in the passage, development of improved memory technology is IMPORTANT because    24.____

    A. it demonstrates the feasibility of associative processors
    B. memory represents one of the chief limitations on computer performance today
    C. semiconductors are expected to largely replace core which now represents about half of the memory market
    D. data can now be speeded through the use of CAM

25. Three types of memory media which are discussed in the above passage are    25.____

    A. core, plated wire, semiconductors
    B. high speed buffer, magnetic disks, rotating magnetic storage
    C. ferrite cores, magnetic drums, remote data terminals
    D. high speed buffers, magnetic disks, magnetic drums

# KEY (CORRECT ANSWERS)

| | | | | |
|---|---|---|---|---|
| 1. | C | | 11. | B |
| 2. | B | | 12. | A |
| 3. | A | | 13. | A |
| 4. | B | | 14. | D |
| 5. | A | | 15. | A |
| | | | | |
| 6. | D | | 16. | D |
| 7. | D | | 17. | D |
| 8. | D | | 18. | D |
| 9. | A | | 19. | D |
| 10. | C | | 20. | D |

| | |
|---|---|
| 21. | B |
| 22. | D |
| 23. | A |
| 24. | B |
| 25. | A |

# TEST 2

DIRECTIONS: Each question or incomplete statement is followed by several suggested answers or completions. Select the one that BEST answers the question or completes the statement. *PRINT THE LETTER OF THE CORRECT ANSWER IN THE SPACE AT THE RIGHT.*

Questions 1-5.

DIRECTIONS: Questions 1 through 5 are to be answered SOLELY on the basis of the following paragraph.

Work standards presuppose an ability to measure work. Measurement in office management is needed for several reasons. First, it is necessary to evaluate the overall efficiency of the office itself. It is then essential to measure the efficiency of each particular section or unit and that of the individual worker. To plan and control the work of sections and units, one must have measurement. A program of measurement goes hand in hand with a program of standards. One can have measurement without standards, but one cannot have work standards without measurement. Providing data on amount of work done and time expended, measurement does not deal with the amount of energy expended by an individual although, in many cases, such energy may be in direct proportion to work output. Usually from two-thirds to three-fourths of all work can be measured. However, less than two-thirds of all work is actually measured because measurement difficulties are encountered when office work is non-repetitive and irregular, or when it is primarily mental rather than manual. These obstacles are often used as excuses for non-measurement far more frequently than is justified.

1. According to the above paragraph, an office manager cannot set work standards unless he can

    A. plan the amount of work to be done
    B. control the amount of work that is done
    C. estimate accurately the quantity of work done
    D. delegate the amount of work to be done to efficient workers

1.____

2. According to the above paragraph, the type of office work that would be MOST difficult to measure would be

    A. checking warrants for accuracy of information
    B. recording payroll changes
    C. processing applications
    D. making up a new system of giving out supplies

2.____

3. According to the above paragraph, the ACTUAL amount of work that is measured is _____ of all work.

    A. less than two-thirds
    B. two-thirds to three-fourths
    C. less than three-sixths
    D. more than three-fourths

3.____

4. Which of the following would be MOST difficult to determine by using measurement techniques?

    A. The amount of work that is accomplished during a certain period of time
    B. The amount of work that should be planned for a period of time
    C. How much time is needed to do a certain task
    D. The amount of incentive a person must have to do his job

4.____

5. The one of the following which is the MOST suitable title for the above paragraph is          5._____

    A. HOW MEASUREMENT OF OFFICE EFFICIENCY DEPENDS ON WORK STAN-DARDS
    B. USING MEASUREMENT FOR OFFICE MANAGEMENT AND EFFICIENCY
    C. WORK STANDARDS AND THE EFFICIENCY OF THE OFFICE WORKER
    D. MANAGING THE OFFICE USING MEASURED WORK STANDARDS

Questions 6-9.

DIRECTIONS:   Questions 6 through 9 are to be answered SOLELY on the basis of the following passage.

    Work measurement concerns accomplishment or productivity. It has to do with results; it does not deal with the amount of energy used up, although in many cases this may be in direct proportion to the work output. Work measurement not only helps a manager to distribute work loads fairly, but it also enables him to define work success in actual units, evaluate employee performance, and determine where corrective help is needed. Work measurement is accomplished by measuring the amount produced, measuring the time spent to produce it, and relating the two. To illustrate, it is common to speak of so many orders processed within a given time. The number of orders processed becomes meaningful when related to the amount of time taken.

    Much of the work in an office can be measured fairly accurately and inexpensively. The extent of work measurement possible in any given case will depend upon the particular type of office tasks performed, but usually from two-thirds to three-fourths of all work in an office can be measured. It is true that difficulty in work measurement is encountered, for example, when the office work is irregular and not repeated often, or when the work is primarily mental rather than manual. These are problems, but they are used as excuses for doing no work measurement far more frequently than is justified.

6. According to the above passage, which of the following BEST illustrates the type of information obtained as a result of work measurement?          6._____

    A. Clerk takes one hour to file 150 folders
    B. Typist types five letters
    C. Stenographer works harder typing from shorthand notes than she does typing from a typed draft
    D. Clerk keeps track of employees' time by computing sick leave, annual leave, and overtime leave

7. The above passage does NOT indicate that work measurement can be used to help a supervisor to determine          7._____

    A. *why* an employee is performing poorly on the job
    B. *who* are the fast and slow workers in the unit
    C. *how* the work in the unit should be divided up
    D. *how* long it should take to perform a certain task

8. According to the above passage, the kind of work that would be MOST difficult to measure would be such work as          8._____

    A. sorting mail
    B. designing a form for a new procedure
    C. photocopying various materials
    D. answering inquiries with form letters

9. The excuses mentioned in the above passage for failure to perform work measurement can be BEST summarized as the 9.____

    A. repetitive nature of office work
    B. costs involved in carrying out accurate work measurement
    C. inability to properly use the results obtained from work measurement
    D. difficulty involved in measuring certain types of work

Questions 10-13.

DIRECTIONS:    Questions 10 through 13 are to be answered SOLELY on the basis of the following passage.

    Job analysis combined with performance appraisal is an excellent method of determining training needs of individuals. The steps in this method are to determine the specific duties of the job, to evaluate the adequacy with which the employee performs each of these duties, and finally to determine what significant improvements can be made by training.

    The list of duties can be obtained in a number of ways: asking the employee, asking the supervisor, observing the employee, etc. Adequacy of performance can be estimated by the employee, but the supervisor's evaluation must also be obtained. This evaluation will usually be based on observation.

    What does the supervisor observe? The employee, while he is working; the employee's work relationships; the ease, speed, and sureness of the employee's actions; the way he applies himself to the job; the accuracy and amount of completed work, its conformity with established procedures and standards; the appearance of the work; the soundness of judgment it shows; and, finally, signs of good or poor communication, understanding, and cooperation among employees.

    Such observation is a normal and inseparable part of the everyday job of supervision. Systematically recorded, evaluated, and summarized, it highlights both general and individual training needs.

10. According to the above passage, job analysis may be used by the supervisor in 10.____

    A. increasing his own understanding of tasks performed in his unit
    B. increasing efficiency of communication within the organization
    C. assisting personnel experts in the classification of positions
    D. determining in which areas an employee needs more instruction

11. According to the above passage, the FIRST step in determining the training needs of employees is to 11.____

    A. locate the significant improvements that can be made by training
    B. determine the specific duties required in a job
    C. evaluate the employee's performance
    D. motivate the employee to want to improve himself

12. On the basis of the above passage, which of the following is the BEST way for a supervi-  12.____
sor to determine the adequacy of employee performance?

    A. Check the accuracy and amount of completed work
    B. Ask the training officer
    C. Observe all aspects of the employee's work
    D. Obtain the employee's own estimate

13. Which of the following is NOT mentioned by the above passage as a factor to be taken  13.____
into consideration in judging the adequacy of employee performance?

    A. Accuracy of completed work
    B. Appearance of completed work
    C. Cooperation among employees
    D. Attitude of the employee toward his supervisor

Questions 14-15.

DIRECTIONS:   Questions 14 and 15 are to be answered SOLELY on the basis of the following
                paragraph.

The fundamental characteristic of the type of remote control which management needs
to bridge the gap between itself and actual operations is the more effective use of records
and reports – more specifically, the gathering and interpretation of the facts contained in
records and reports. Facts, for management purposes, are those data (narrative and quanti-
tative) which express in simple terms the current standing of the agency's program, work, and
resources in relation to the plans and policies formulated by management. They are those
facts or measures (1) which permit management to compare current status with past performance and with its forecasts for the immediate future, and (2) which provide management
with a reliable basis for long-range forecasting.

14. For management purposes, facts are, according to the above paragraph,  14.____

    A. forecasts which can be compared to current status
    B. data which can be used for certain control purposes
    C. a fundamental characteristic of a type of remote control
    D. the data contained in records and reports

15. An inference which can be drawn from this statement is that  15.____

    A. management which has a reliable basis for long-range forecasting has at its dis-
       posal a type of remote control which is needed to bridge the gap between itself and
       actual operations
    B. data which do not express in simple terms the current standing of the agency's pro-
       gram, work, and resources in relationship to the plans and policies formulated by
       management may still be facts for management purposes
    C. data which express relationships among the agency's program, work, and
       resources are management facts
    D. the gap between management and actual operations can only be bridged by char-
       acteristics which are fundamentally a type of remote control

Questions 16-17.

DIRECTIONS:   Questions 16 and 17 are to be answered SOLELY on the basis of the following
passage.

Two approaches are available in developing criteria for the evaluation of plans. One
approach, designated <u>Approach A</u>, is a review and analysis of characteristics that differenti-
ate successful plans from unsuccessful plans. These criteria are descriptive in nature and
serve as a checklist against which the plan under consideration may be judged. These characteristics have been observed by many different students of planning, and there is considerable agreement concerning the characteristics necessary for a plan to be successful.

A second approach to the development of criteria for judging plans, designated
<u>Approach B</u>, is the determination of the degree to which the plan under consideration is eco-
nomic. The word *economic* is used here in its broadest sense; i.e., effective in its utilization of
resources. In order to determine the economic worth of a plan, it is necessary to use a technique that permits the description of any plan in economic terms and to utilize this technique
to the extent that it becomes a *way of thinking* about plans.

16.   According to <u>Approach B</u>, the MOST successful plan is *generally* one which                16._____

    A.   costs least to implement
    B.   gives most value for resources expended
    C.   uses the least expensive resources
    D.   utilizes the greatest number of resources

17.   According to <u>Approach A</u>, a successful plan is one which is                17._____

    A.   descriptive in nature
    B.   lowest in cost
    C.   similar to other successful plans
    D.   agreed upon by many students of planning

Questions 18-20.

DIRECTIONS:   Questions 18 through 20 are to be answered SOLELY on the basis of the following passage.

The primary purpose of control reports is to supply information intended to serve as the
basis for corrective action if needed. At the same time, the significance of control reports
must be kept in proper perspective. Control reports are only a part of the planning-manage-
ment information system. Control information includes nonfinancial as well as financial data
that measure performance and isolate variances from standard. Control information also provides feedback so that planning information may be updated and corrected. Whenever possible, control reports should be designed so that they provide feedback for the planning
process as well as provide information of immediate value to the control process.

Since the culmination of the control process is the taking of necessary corrective action
to bring performance in line with standards, it follows that control information must be directed
to the person who is organizationally responsible for taking the required action. Usually the
same information, though in a somewhat abbreviated form, is given to the responsible man-

ager's superior. A district sales manager needs a complete daily record of the performance of each of his salesmen; yet, the report forwarded to the regional sales manager summarizes only the performance of each sales district in his region. In preparing reports for higher echelons of management, summary statements and recommendations for action should appear on the first page; substantiating data, usually the information presented to the person directly responsible for the operation, may be included if needed.

18. A control report serves its primary purpose as part of the process which leads DIRECTLY to

    A. better planning for future action
    B. increasing the performance of district salesmen
    C. the establishment of proper performance standards
    D. taking corrective action when performance is poor

18.____

19. The one of the following which would be the BEST description of a control report is that a control report is a form of

    A. planning              B. communication
    C. direction             D. organization

19.____

20. If control reports are to be effective, the one of the following which is LEAST essential to the effectiveness of control reporting is a system of

    A. communication         B. standards
    C. authority             D. work simplification

20.____

Questions 21-23.

DIRECTIONS: Questions 21 through 23 are to be answered SOLELY on the basis of the following passage.

The need for the best in management techniques has given rise to the expression *scientific management*. Within reasonable limits, management can be scientific, but it will probably be many decades before it becomes truly scientific either in the factory or in the office. As long as it is impossible to measure accurately individual performance and to equate human behavior, so long will it be impossible to develop completely scientific techniques of office management. There is a likelihood, of course, that management might be reduced to a science when it is applied to inanimate objects which facilitate operations such as machinery, office equipment and furnishings, and forms. The limiting factor, therefore, is the human element.

21. The above passage is concerned PRIMARILY with the

    A. value of scientific office management
    B. methods for the development of scientific office management
    C. need for the best office management techniques
    D. possibility of reducing office management to a science

21.____

22. According to the above passage, the realization of truly scientific office management is dependent upon the

    A. expression of management techniques
    B. development of accurate personnel measurement techniques

22.____

C.  passage of many decades, most probably
D.  elimination of individual differences in human behavior

23.  According to the above passage, the scientific management of inanimate objects                     23.____

A.  occurs automatically because there is no human factor
B.  cannot occur in a factory, but can occur in an office
C.  could be achieved without the concurrent achievement of truly scientific office management
D.  is not a necessary component of truly scientific office management

Questions 24-25.

DIRECTIONS:   Questions 24 and 25 are to be answered SOLELY on the basis of the following paragraph.

Your role as human resources utilization experts is to submit your techniques to operating administrators, for the program must, in reality, be theirs, not yours. We, in personnel, have been guilty of encouraging operating executives to believe that these important matters affecting their employees are personnel department matters, not management matters. We should hardly be surprised, as a consequence, to find these executives playing down the role of personnel and finding personnel routines a nuisance, for these are not in the mainstream of managing the enterprise – or so we have encouraged them to believe.

24.  The BEST of the following interpretations of the above paragraph is that                     24.____

A.  personnel people have been guilty of *passing the buck* on personnel functions
B.  operating officials have difficulty understanding personnel techniques
C.  personnel employees have tended to usurp some functions rightfully belonging to management
D.  matters affecting employees should be handled by the personnel department

25.  The BEST of the following interpretations of the above paragraph is that                     25.____

A.  personnel departments have aided and abetted the formulation of negative attitudes on the part of management
B.  personnel people are labor relations experts and should carry out these duties
C.  personnel activities are not really the responsibility of management
D.  management is now being encouraged by personnel experts to assume some responsibility for personnel functions

# KEY (CORRECT ANSWERS)

1. C
2. D
3. A
4. D
5. B

6. A
7. A
8. B
9. D
10. D

11. B
12. C
13. D
14. B
15. C

16. B
17. C
18. D
19. B
20. D

21. D
22. B
23. C
24. C
25. A

# TEST 3

DIRECTIONS: Each question or incomplete statement is followed by several suggested answers or completions. Select the one that BEST answers the question or completes the statement. *PRINT THE LETTER OF THE CORRECT ANSWER IN THE SPACE AT THE RIGHT.*

Questions 1-3

DIRECTIONS: Questions 1 through 3 are to be answered SOLELY on the basis of the following paragraph.

Prior to revising its child care program, a department feels that it is necessary to get some information from the mothers served by the existing program in order to determine where changes are required. A questionnaire is to be constructed to obtain this information.

1. Of the following points which can be taken into consideration in the construction of the questionnaire, the one which is of LEAST importance is 1.____

   A. that the data are to be put into punch cards
   B. the aspects of the program which seem to be in need of change
   C. the type of person who will fill out the questionnaire
   D. testing the questionnaire for ambiguity in advance of general distribution
   E. setting up a control group so that answers received can be compared to a standard

2. To discuss this questionnaire with all mothers who have been asked to answer it, before they actually fill it out, is 2.____

   A. *desirable;* the mothers may be able to offer valuable suggestions for changes in the form of the questionnaire
   B. *undesirable;* it is of some value but consumes too much valuable time
   C. *desirable;* cooperation and uniform interpretation will tend to be achieved
   D. *undesirable;* it may cause the answers to be biased
   E. *desirable;* the group will tend to support the program

3. Of the following items included in the questionnaire, the one which will be of LEAST assistance for comparing attitudes toward the program among different kinds of persons is 3.____

   A. name        B. address        C. age
   D. place of birth    E. education

Questions 4-6.

DIRECTIONS: Questions 4 through 6 are to be answered SOLELY on the basis of the following paragraph.

The supervisor of a large clerical and statistical division has assigned to one of the units under his supervision the preparation of a special statistical report required by the department head. The unit head accepted the assignment without comment but soon ran into considerable difficulty because no one in his unit had had any statistical training.

4. If a result of this lack of training is that the report is not completed on time, although everyone has done all that could be expected, the responsibility for the failure rests with 4.____

   A. the department head        B. the supervisor
   C. the unit head              D. the employees in the unit
   E. no one

5. This incident indicates that the supervisory staff has insufficient knowledge of employee     5.____

    A. capabilities
    B. reaction to increased demands
    C. on-the-job training needs
    D. work habits
    E. ability to perform ordinary assignments

6. After working on the report for two days, the unit head notifies the supervisor that he will     6.____
not be able to get the report out in the required time. He states that his staff will be completely trained in another day or two and that after that preparing the report will be a simple matter. At this stage, the supervisor decides to have the statistical unit prepare the report. This action on the part of the supervisor is

    A. *undesirable;* the unit head should be given an incentive to continue with his training program which may produce good results
    B. *desirable;* it is the most effective way in which the supervisor can show his displeasure with the unit head's failure
    C. *undesirable;* it may adversely affect the morale of the unit
    D. *desirable;* it will generally result in a better report completed in a shorter time
    E. *undesirable;* the time spent on training the unit will be completely wasted

Questions 7-9.

DIRECTIONS:   Questions 7 through 9 are to be answered SOLELY on the basis of the following paragraph.

The regressive uses of discipline are ubiquitous. Administrative architects who seek the optimum balance between structure and morale must accordingly look toward the identification and isolation of disciplinary elements. The whole range of disciplinary sanctions, from the reprimand to the dismissal, presents opportunities for reciprocity and accommodation of institutional interests. When rightly seized upon, these opportunities may provide the moment and the means for fruitful exercise of leadership and collaboration.

7. The one of the following ways of reworking the ideas presented in the above paragraph in     7.____
order to be BEST suited for presentation in an in-service training course in supervision is:

    A. When one of your men does something wrong, talk it over with him. Tell him what he should have done. This is a chance for you to show the man that you are on his side and that you would welcome him on your side.
    B. It is not necessary to reprimand or to dismiss an employee because he needs disciplining. The alert foreman will lead and collaborate with his subordinates, making discipline unnecessary.
    C. A good way to lead the men you supervise is to take those opportunities which present themselves to use the whole range of disciplinary sanctions from reprimand to dismissal as a means for enforcing collaboration.
    D. Chances to punish a man in your squad should be welcomed as opportunities to show that you are a *good guy* who does not bear a grudge.
    E. Before you talk to a man or have him report to the office for something he has done wrong, attempt to lead him and get him to work with you. Tell him that his actions were wrong, that you expect him not to repeat the same wrong act, and that you will take a firmer stand if the act is repeated.

8. Of the following, the PRINCIPAL point made in the paragraph above is that  8._____

    A. discipline is frequently used improperly
    B. it is possible to isolate the factors entering into a disciplinary situation
    C. identification of the disciplinary elements is desirable
    D. disciplinary situations may be used to the advantage of the organization
    E. obtaining the best relationship between organizational form and spirit depends upon the ability to label disciplinary elements

9. The MOST novel idea presented in the above paragraph is that  9._____

    A. discipline is rarely necessary
    B. discipline may be a joint action of man and supervisor
    C. there are disciplinary elements which may be identified
    D. a range of disciplinary sanctions exists
    E. it is desirable to seek for balance between structure and morale.

Questions 10-11.

DIRECTIONS:   Questions 10 and 11 are to be answered SOLELY on the basis of the following paragraph.

    People must be selected to do the tasks involved and must be placed on a payroll in jobs fairly priced. Each of these people must be assigned those tasks which he can perform best; the work of each must be appraised, and good and poor work singled out appropriately. Skill in performing assigned tasks must be developed, and the total work situation must be conducive to sustained high performance. Finally, employees must be separated from the work force either voluntarily or involuntarily because of inefficient or unsatisfactory performance or because of curtailment of organizational activities.

10. A personnel function which is NOT included in the above description is  10._____

    A. classification      B. training      C. placement
    D. severance        E. service rating

11. The underlying implied purpose of the policy enunciated in the above paragraph is  11._____

    A. to plan for the curtailment of the organizational program when it becomes necessary
    B. to single out appropriate skill in performing assigned tasks
    C. to develop and maintain a high level of performance by employees
    D. that training employees in relation to the total work situation is essential if good and poor work are to be singled out
    E. that equal money for equal work results in a total work situation which insures proper appraisal

Questions 12-16.

DIRECTIONS:   Questions 12 through 16 are to be answered SOLELY on the basis of the following sections which appeared in a report on the work production of two bureaus of a department. Throughout the report, assume that each month has 4 weeks.

Each of the two bureaus maintains a chronological file. In Bureau A, every 9 months on the average, this material fills a standard legal size file cabinet sufficient for 12,000 work units. In Bureau B, the same type of cabinet is filled in 18 months. Each bureau maintains three complete years of information plus a current file. When the current file cabinet is filled, the cabinet containing the oldest material is emptied, the contents disposed of, and the cabinet used for current material. The similarity of these operations makes it possible to consolidate these files with little effort.

Study of the practice of using typists as filing clerks for periods when there is no typing work showed (1) Bureau A has for the past 6 months completed a total of 1500 filing work units a week using on the average 200 man-hours of trained file clerk time and 20 man-hours of typist time, (2) Bureau B has in the same period completed a total of 2000 filing work units a week using on the average 125 man-hours of trained file clerk time and 60 hours of typist time. This includes all work in chronological files. Assuming that all clerks work at the same speed and that all typists work at the same speed, this indicates that work other than filing should be found for typists or that they should be given some training in the filing procedures used.... It should be noted that Bureau A has not been producing the 1,600 units of technical (not filing) work per 30 day period required by Schedule K, but is at present 200 units behind. The Bureau should be allowed 3 working days to get on schedule.

12. What percentage (approximate) of the total number of filing work units completed in both units consists of the work involved in the maintenance of the chronological files?

    A.  5%      B.  10%      C.  15%      D.  20%      E.  25%

12.____

13. If the two chronological files are consolidated, the number of months which should be allowed for filling a cabinet is

    A.  2      B.  4      C.  6      D.  8      E.  14

13.____

14. The MAXIMUM number of file cabinets which can be released for other uses as a result of the consolidation recommended is

    A.  0
    B.  1
    C.  2
    D.  3
    E.  not determinable on the basis of the data given

14.____

15. If all the filing work for both units is consolidated without any diminution in the amount to be done and all filing work is done by trained file clerks, the number of clerks required (35-hour work week) is

    A.  4      B.  5      C.  6      D.  7      E.  8

15.____

16. In order to comply with the recommendation with respect to Schedule K, the present work production of Bureau A must be increased by

    A.  50%            B.  100%
    C.  150%          D.  200%
    E.  an amount which is not determinable on the basis of the data given

16.____

Questions 17-18.

DIRECTIONS:   Questions 17 and 18 are to be answered SOLELY on the basis of the following paragraph.

Production planning is mainly a process of synthesis. As a basis for the positive act of bringing complex production elements properly together, however, analysis is necessary, especially if improvement is to be made in an existing organization. The necessary analysis requires customary means of orientation and preliminary fact gathering with emphasis, however, on the recognition of administrative goals and of the relationship among work steps.

17.   The entire process described is PRIMARILY one of                                          17.____

    A.   taking apart, examining, and recombining
    B.   deciding what changes are necessary, making the changes and checking on their value
    C.   fact finding so as to provide the necessary orientation
    D.   discovering just where the emphasis in production should be placed and then modifying the existing procedure so that it is placed properly
    E.   recognizing administrative goals and the relationship among work steps

18.   In production planning, according to the above paragraph, analysis is used PRIMARILY    18.____
      as

    A.   a means of making important changes in an organization
    B.   the customary means of orientation and preliminary fact finding
    C.   a development of the relationship among work steps
    D.   a means for holding the entire process intact by providing a logical basis
    E.   a method to obtain the facts upon which a theory can be built

Questions 19-21.

DIRECTIONS:   Questions 19 through 21 are to be answered SOLELY on the basis of the following paragraph.

Public administration is policy-making. But it is not autonomous, exclusive, or isolated policy-making. It is policy-making on a field where mighty forces contend, forces engendered in and by society. It is policy-making subject to still other and various policy makers. Public administration is one of a number of basic political processes by which these people achieve and control government.

19.   From the point of view expressed in the above paragraph, public administration is          19.____

    A.   becoming a technical field with completely objective processes
    B.   the primary force in modern society
    C.   a technical field which should be divorced from the actual decision-making function
    D.   basically anti-democratic
    E.   intimately related to politics

20. According to the above paragraph, public administration is NOT entirely          20.____

    A. a force generated in and by society
    B. subject at times to controlling influences
    C. a social process
    D. policy-making relating to administrative practices
    E. related to policy-making at lower levels

21. The above paragraph asserts that public administration          21.____

    A. develops the basic and controlling policies
    B. is the result of policies made by many different forces
    C. should attempt to break through its isolated policymaking and engage on a broader field
    D. is a means of directing government
    E. is subject to the political processes by which acts are controlled

Questions 22-24.

DIRECTIONS:   Questions 22 through 24 are to be answered SOLELY on the basis of the following paragraph.

    In order to understand completely the source of an employee's insecurity on his job, it is necessary to understand how he came to be, who he is, and what kind of a person he is away from his job. This would necessitate an understanding of those personal assets and liabilities which the employee brings to the job situation. These arise from his individual characteristics and his past experiences and established patterns of interpersonal relations. This whole area is of tremendous scope, encompassing everything included within the study of psychiatry and interpersonal relations. Therefore, it has been impracticable to consider it in detail. Attention has been focused on the relatively circumscribed area of the actual occupational situation. The factors considered – those which the employee brings to the job situation and which arise from his individual characteristics and his past experience and established patterns of interpersonal relations – are: intellectual level or capacity, specific aptitudes, education, work experience, health, social and economic background, patterns of interpersonal relations and resultant personality characteristics.

22. According to the above paragraph, the one of the following fields of study which would be          22.____
of LEAST importance in the study of the problem is the

    A. relationships existing among employees
    B. causes of employee insecurity in the job situation
    C. conflict, if it exists, between intellectual level and work experience
    D. distribution of intellectual achievement
    E. relationship between employee characteristics and the established pattern of interpersonal relations in the work situation

23. According to the above paragraph, in order to make a thoroughgoing and comprehensive          23.____
study of the sources of employee insecurity, the field of study should include

    A. only such circumscribed areas as are involved in extra-occupational situations
    B. a study of the dominant mores of the period
    C. all branches of the science of psychology

D.  a determination of the characteristics, such as intellectual capacity, which an employee should bring to the job situation
E.  employee personality characteristics arising from previous relationships with other people

24. It is implied by the above paragraph that it would be of GREATEST advantage to bring to this problem a comprehensive knowledge of 24.____

A.  all established patterns of interpersonal relations
B.  the milieu in which the employee group is located
C.  what assets and liabilities are presented in the job situation
D.  methods of focusing attention on relatively circumscribed regions
E.  the sources of an employee's insecurity on his job

Questions 25-26.

DIRECTIONS:   Questions 25 and 26 are to be answered SOLELY on the basis of the following paragraph.

If, during a study, some hundreds of values of a variable (such as annual number of late-nesses for each employee in a department) have been noted merely in the arbitrary order in which they happen to occur, the mind cannot properly grasp the significance of the record; the observations must be ranked or classified in some way before the characteristics of the series can be comprehended, and those comparisons, on which arguments as to causation depend, can be made with other series. A dichotomous classification is too crude; if the values are merely classified according to whether they exceed or fall short of some fixed value, a large part of the information given by the original record is lost. Numerical measurements lend themselves with peculiar readiness to a manifold classification.

25. According to the above paragraph, if the values of a variable which are gathered during a study are classified in a few subdivisions, the MOST likely result will be 25.____

A.  an inability to grasp the significance of the record
B.  an inability to relate the series with other series
C.  a loss of much of the information in the original data
D.  a loss of the readiness with which numerical measurements lend themselves to a manifold classification
E.  that the order in which they happen to occur will be arbitrary

26. The above paragraph advocates, with respect to numerical data, the use of 26.____

A.  arbitrary order
B.  comparisons with other series
C.  a two value classification
D.  a many value classification
E.  all values of a variable

Question 27.

DIRECTIONS: Question 27 is to be answered SOLELY on the basis of the following paragraph.

A more significant manifestation of the concern of the community with the general welfare is the collection and dissemination of statistics. This statement may cause the reader to smile, for statistics seem to be drab and prosaic things. The great growth of statistics, however, is one of the most remarkable characteristics of the age. Never before has a community kept track from month to month, and in some cases from week to week, of how many people are born, how many die and from what causes, how many are sick, how much is being produced, how much is being sold, how many people are at work, how many people are unemployed, how long they have been out of work, what prices people pay, how much income they receive and from what sources, how much they owe, what they intend to buy. These elaborate attempts of the country to keep informed about what is happening mean that the community is concerned with how its members are faring and with the conditions under which they live. For this reason, the present age may take pride in its numerous and regular statistical reports and in the rapid increase in the number of these reports. No other age has evidenced such a keen interest in the conditions of the people.

27.  The writer implies that statistics are                                                 27.____

    A.  too scientific for general use
    B.  too elaborate and too drab
    C.  related to the improvement of living conditions
    D.  frequently misinterpreted
    E.  a product of the machine age

--------

# KEY (CORRECT ANSWERS)

| | | | | |
|---|---|---|---|---|
| 1. | E | | 11. | C |
| 2. | C | | 12. | C |
| 3. | A | | 13. | C |
| 4. | B | | 14. | B |
| 5. | A | | 15. | D |
| 6. | D | | 16. | E |
| 7. | A | | 17. | A |
| 8. | D | | 18. | E |
| 9. | B | | 19. | E |
| 10. | A | | 20. | D |

| | |
|---|---|
| 21. | D |
| 22. | D |
| 23. | E |
| 24. | B |
| 25. | C |
| 26. | D |
| 27. | C |

--------

# GLOSSARY OF COMPUTER TERMS

## Contents

# GLOSSARY OF COMPUTER TERMS

## Basic

**application & app**

An application (often called "app" for short) is simply a program with a GUI. Note that it is different from an applet.

**boot**

Starting up an OS is booting it. If the computer is already running, it is more often called rebooting.

**browser**

A browser is a program used to browse the web. Some common browsers include Netscape, MSIE (Microsoft Internet Explorer), Safari, Lynx, Mosaic, Amaya, Arena, Chimera, Opera, Cyberdog, HotJava, etc.

**bug**

A bug is a mistake in the design of something, especially software. A really severe bug can cause something to crash.

**chat**

Chatting is like e-mail, only it is done instantaneously and can directly involve multiple people at once. While e-mail now relies on one more or less standard protocol, chatting still has a couple competing ones. Of particular note are IRC and Instant Messenger. One step beyond chatting is called MUDding.

**click**

To press a mouse button. When done twice in rapid succession, it is referred to as a double-click.

**cursor**

A point of attention on the computer screen, often marked with a flashing line or block. Text typed into the computer will usually appear at the cursor.

**database**

A database is a collection of data, typically organized to make common retrievals easy and efficient. Some common database programs include Oracle, Sybase, Postgres, Informix, Filemaker, Adabas, etc.

**desktop**

A desktop system is a computer designed to sit in one position on a desk somewhere and not move around. Most general purpose computers are desktop systems. Calling a system a desktop implies nothing about its platform. The fastest desktop system at any given time is typically either an Alpha or PowerPC based system, but the SPARC and PA-RISC based systems are also often in the running. Industrial strength desktops are typically called workstations.

**directory**

Also called "folder", a directory is a collection of files typically created for organizational purposes. Note that a directory is itself a file, so a directory can generally contain other directories. It differs in this way from a partition.

**disk**

A disk is a physical object used for storing data. It will not forget its data when it loses power. It is always used in conjunction with a disk drive. Some disks can be removed from their drives, some cannot. Generally it is possible to write new information to a disk in addition to reading data from it, but this is not always the case.

**drive**

A device for storing and/or retrieving data. Some drives (such as disk drives, zip drives, and tape drives) are typically capable of having new data written to them, but some others (like CD-ROMs or DVD-ROMs) are not. Some drives have random access (like disk drives, zip drives, CD-ROMs, and DVD-ROMs), while others only have sequential access (like tape drives).

**e-book**

The concept behind an e-book is that it should provide all the functionality of an ordinary book but in a manner that is (overall) less expensive and more environmentally friendly. The actual term e-book is somewhat confusingly used to refer to a variety of things: custom software to play e-book titles, dedicated hardware to play e-book titles, and the e-book titles themselves. Individual e-book titles can be free or commercial (but will always be less expensive than their printed counterparts) and have to be loaded into a player to be read. Players vary wildly in capability level. Basic ones allow simple reading and bookmarking; better ones include various features like hypertext, illustrations, audio, and even limited video. Other optional features allow the user to mark-up sections of text, leave notes, circle or diagram things, highlight passages, program or customize settings, and even use interactive fiction. There are many types of e-book; a couple popular ones include the Newton book and Palm DOC.

**e-mail**

E-mail is short for electronic mail. It allows for the transfer of information from one computer to another, provided that they are hooked up via some sort of network (often the Internet. E-mail works similarly to FAXing, but its contents typically get printed out on the other end only on demand, not immediately and automatically as with FAX. A machine receiving e-mail will also not reject other incoming mail messages as a busy FAX machine will; rather they will instead be queued up to be received after the current batch has been completed. E-mail is only seven-bit clean, meaning that you should not expect anything other than ASCII data to go through uncorrupted without prior conversion via something like uucode or bcode. Some mailers will do some conversion automatically, but unless you know your mailer is one of them, you may want to do the encoding manually.

**file**

A file is a unit of (usually named) information stored on a computer.

**firmware**

Sort of in-between hardware and software, firmware consists of modifiable programs embedded in hardware. Firmware updates should be treated with care since they can literally destroy the underlying hardare if done improperly. There are also cases where neglecting to apply a firmware update can destroy the underlying hardware, so user beware.

**floppy**

An extremely common type of removable disk. Floppies do not hold too much data, but most computers are capable of reading them. Note though that there are different competing format used for floppies, so that a floppy written by one type of computer might not directly work on another. Also sometimes called "diskette".

**format**

The manner in which data is stored; its organization. For example, VHS, SVHS, and Beta are three different formats of video tape. They are not 100% compatible with each other, but information can be transferred from one to the other with the proper equipment (but not always without loss; SVHS contains more information than either of the other two). Computer information can be stored in literally hundreds of different formats, and can represent text, sounds, graphics, animations, etc. Computer information can be exchanged via different computer types provided both computers can interpret the format used.

**function keys**

On a computer keyboard, the keys that start with an "F" that are usually (but not always) found on the top row. They are meant to perform user-defined tasks.

**graphics**
Anything visually displayed on a computer that is not text.
**hardware**
The physical portion of the computer.
**hypertext**
A hypertext document is like a text document with the ability to contain pointers to other regions of (possibly other) hypertext documents.
**Internet**
The Internet is the world-wide network of computers. There is only one Internet, and thus it is typically capitalized (although it is sometimes referred to as "the 'net"). It is different from an intranet.
**keyboard**
A keyboard on a computer is almost identical to a keyboard on a typewriter. Computer keyboards will typically have extra keys, however. Some of these keys (common examples include Control, Alt, and Meta) are meant to be used in conjunction with other keys just like shift on a regular typewriter. Other keys (common examples include Insert, Delete, Home, End, Help, function keys,etc.) are meant to be used independently and often perform editing tasks. Keyboards on different platforms will often look slightly different and have somewhat different collections of keys. Some keyboards even have independent shift lock and caps lock keys. Smaller keyboards with only math-related keys are typically called "keypads".
**language**
Computer programs can be written in a variety of different languages. Different languages are optimized for different tasks. Common languages include Java, C, C++, ForTran, Pascal, Lisp, and BASIC. Some people classify languages into two categories, higher-level and lower-level. These people would consider assembly language and machine language lower-level languages and all other languages higher-level. In general, higher-level languages can be either interpreted or compiled; many languages allow both, but some are restricted to one or the other. Many people do not consider machine language and assembly language at all when talking about programming languages.
**laptop**
A laptop is any computer designed to do pretty much anything a desktop system can do but run for a short time (usually two to five hours) on batteries. They are designed to be carried around but are not particularly convenient to carry around. They are significantly more expensive than desktop systems and have far worse battery life than PDAs. Calling a system a laptop implies nothing about its platform. By far the fastest laptops are the PowerPC based Macintoshes.
**memory**
Computer memory is used to temporarily store data. In reality, computer memory is only capable of remembering sequences of zeros and ones, but by utilizing the binary number system it is possible to produce arbitrary rational numbers and through clever formatting all manner of representations of pictures, sounds, and animations. The most common types of memory are RAM, ROM, and flash.
**MHz & megahertz**
One megahertz is equivalent to 1000 kilohertz, or 1,000,000 hertz. The clock speed of the main processor of many computers is measured in MHz, and is sometimes (quite misleadingly) used to represent the overall speed of a computer. In fact, a computer's speed is based upon many factors, and since MHz only reveals how many clock cycles the main processor has per second (saying nothing about how much is actually accomplished per cycle), it can really only accurately be used to gauge two computers with the same generation and family of processor plus similar configurations of memory, co-processors, and other peripheral hardware.
**modem**
A modem allows two computers to communicate over ordinary phone lines. It derives its name

from **mod**ulate / **dem**odulate, the process by which it converts digital computer data back and forth for use with an analog phone line.

**monitor**

The screen for viewing computer information is called a monitor.

**mouse**

In computer parlance a mouse can be both the physical object moved around to control a pointer on the screen, and the pointer itself. Unlike the animal, the proper plural of computer mouse is "mouses".

**multimedia**

This originally indicated a capability to work with and integrate various types of things including audio, still graphics, and especially video. Now it is more of a marketing term and has little real meaning. Historically the Amiga was the first multimedia machine. Today in addition to AmigaOS, IRIX and Solaris are popular choices for high-end multimedia work.

**NC**

The term **n**etwork **c**omputer refers to any (usually desktop) computer system that is designed to work as part of a network rather than as a stand-alone machine. This saves money on hardware, software, and maintenance by taking advantage of facilities already available on the network. The term "Internet appliance" is often used interchangeably with NC.

**network**

A network (as applied to computers) typically means a group of computers working together. It can also refer to the physical wire etc. connecting the computers.

**notebook**

A notebook is a small laptop with similar price, performance, and battery life.

**organizer**

An organizer is a tiny computer used primarily to store names, addresses, phone numbers, and date book information. They usually have some ability to exchange information with desktop systems. They boast even better battery life than PDAs but are far less capable. They are extremely inexpensive but are typically incapable of running any special purpose applications and are thus of limited use.

**OS**

The **o**perating **s**ystem is the program that manages a computer's resources. Common OSes include Windows '95, MacOS, Linux, Solaris, AmigaOS, AIX, Windows NT, etc.

**PC**

The term **p**ersonal **c**omputer properly refers to any desktop, laptop, or notebook computer system. Its use is inconsistent, though, and some use it to specifically refer to x86 based systems running MS-DOS, MS-Windows, GEOS, or OS/2. This latter use is similar to what is meant by a WinTel system.

**PDA**

A **p**ersonal **d**igital **a**ssistant is a small battery-powered computer intended to be carried around by the user rather than left on a desk. This means that the processor used ought to be power-efficient as well as fast, and the OS ought to be optimized for hand-held use. PDAs typically have an instant-on feature (they would be useless without it) and most are grayscale rather than color because of battery life issues. Most have a pen interface and come with a detachable stylus. None use mouses. All have some ability to exchange data with desktop systems. In terms of raw capabilities, a PDA is more capable than an organizer and less capable than a laptop (although some high-end PDAs beat out some low-end laptops). By far the most popular PDA is the Pilot, but other common types include Newtons, Psions, Zauri, Zoomers, and Windows CE hand-helds. By far the fastest current PDA is the Newton (based around a StrongARM RISC processor). Other PDAs are optimized for other tasks; few computers are as personal as PDAs and care must be taken in their purchase. Feneric's PDA / Handheld Comparison Page is perhaps the most detailed comparison of PDAs and handheld computers to be found anywhere on the web.

**platform**

Roughly speaking, a platform represents a computer's family. It is defined by both the processor type on the hardware side and the OS type on the software side. Computers belonging to different platforms cannot typically run each other's programs (unless the programs are written in a language like Java).

**portable**

If something is portable it can be easily moved from one type of computer to another. The verb "to port" indicates the moving itself.

**printer**

A printer is a piece of hardware that will print computer information onto paper.

**processor**

The processor (also called central processing unit, or CPU) is the part of the computer that actually works with the data and runs the programs. There are two main processor types in common usage today: CISC and RISC. Some computers have more than one processor and are thus called "multiprocessor". This is distinct from multitasking. Advertisers often use megahertz numbers as a means of showing a processor's speed. This is often extremely misleading; megahertz numbers are more or less meaningless when compared across different types of processors.

**program**

A program is a series of instructions for a computer, telling it what to do or how to behave. The terms "application" and "app" mean almost the same thing (albeit applications generally have GUIs). It is however different from an applet. Program is also the verb that means to create a program, and a programmer is one who programs.

**run**

Running a program is how it is made to do something. The term "execute" means the same thing.

**software**

The non-physical portion of the computer; the part that exists only as data; the programs. Another term meaning much the same is "code".

**spreadsheet**

An program used to perform various calculations. It is especially popular for financial applications. Some common spreadsheets include Lotus 123, Excel, OpenOffice Spreadsheet, Octave, Gnumeric, AppleWorks Spreadsheet, Oleo, and GeoCalc.

**user**

The operator of a computer.

**word processor**

A program designed to help with the production of textual documents, like letters and memos. Heavier duty work can be done with a desktop publisher. Some common word processors include MS-Word, OpenOffice Write, WordPerfect, AbiWord, AppleWorks Write, and GeoWrite.

**www**

The World-Wide-Web refers more or less to all the publically accessable documents on the Internet. It is used quite loosely, and sometimes indicates only HTML files and sometimes FTP and Gopher files, too. It is also sometimes just referred to as "the web".

## Reference

**65xx**

The 65xx series of processors includes the 6502, 65C02, 6510, 8502, 65C816, 65C816S, etc. It is a CISC design and is not being used in too many new stand-alone computer systems, but is still being used in embedded systems, game systems (such as the Super NES), and processor enhancement add-ons for older systems. It was originally designed by MOS Technologies, but is now produced by The Western Design Center, Inc. It was the primary processor for many extremely popular systems no longer being produced, including the Commodore 64, the Commodore 128, and all the Apple ][ series machines.

**68xx**

The 68xx series of processors includes the 6800, 6805, 6809, 68000, 68020, 68030, 68040, 68060, etc. It is a CISC design and is not being used in too many new stand-alone computer systems, but is still being used heavily in embedded systems. It was originally designed by Motorola and was the primary processor for older generations of many current machines, including Macintoshes, Amigas, Sun workstations, HP workstations, etc. and the primary processor for many systems no longer being produced, such as the TRS-80. The PowerPC was designed in part to be its replacement.

**a11y**

Commonly used to abbreviate the word "accessibility". There are eleven letters between the "a" and the "y".

**ADA**

An object-oriented language at one point popular for military and some academic software. Lately C++ and Java have been getting more attention.

**AI**

Artificial intelligence is the concept of making computers do tasks once considered to require thinking. AI makes computers play chess, recognize handwriting and speech, helps suggest prescriptions to doctors for patients based on imput symptoms, and many other tasks, both mundane and not.

**AIX**

The industrial strength OS designed by IBM to run on PowerPC and x86 based machines. It is a variant of UNIX and is meant to provide more power than OS/2.

**AJaX**

AJaX is a little like DHTML, but it adds asynchronous communication between the browser and Web site via either XML or JSON to achieve performance that often rivals desktop applications.

**Alpha**

An Alpha is a RISC processor invented by Digital and currently produced by Digital/Compaq and Samsung. A few different OSes run on Alpha based machines including Digital UNIX, Windows NT, Linux, NetBSD, and AmigaOS. Historically, at any given time, the fastest processor in the world has usually been either an Alpha or a PowerPC (with sometimes SPARCs and PA-RISCs making the list), but Compaq has recently announced that there will be no further development of this superb processor instead banking on the release of the somewhat suspect Merced.

**AltiVec**

AltiVec (also called the "Velocity Engine") is a special extension built into some PowerPC CPUs to provide better performance for certain operations, most notably graphics and sound. It is similar to MMX on the x86 CPUs. Like MMX, it requires special software for full performance benefits to be realized.

**Amiga**

A platform originally created and only produced by Commodore, but now owned by Gateway 2000 and produced by it and a few smaller companies. It was historically the first multimedia machine and gave the world of computing many innovations. It is now primarily used for audio / video applications; in fact, a decent Amiga system is less expensive than a less capable video editing system. Many music videos were created on Amigas, and a few television series and movies had their special effects generated on Amigas. Also, Amigas can be readily synchronized with video cameras, so typically when a computer screen appears on television or in a movie and it is not flickering wildly, it is probably an Amiga in disguise. Furthermore, many coin-operated arcade games are really Amigas packaged in stand-up boxes. Amigas have AmigaOS for their OS. New Amigas have either a PowerPC or an Alpha for their main processor and a 68xx processor dedicated to graphics manipulation. Older (and low end) Amigas do everything with just a 68xx processor.

## AmigaOS

The OS used by Amigas. AmigaOS combines the functionality of an OS and a window manager and is fully multitasking. AmigaOS boasts a pretty good selection of games (many arcade games are in fact written on Amigas) but has limited driver support. AmigaOS will run on 68xx, Alpha, and PowerPC based machines.

## Apple ][

The Apple ][ computer sold millions of units and is generally considered to have been the first home computer with a 1977 release date. It is based on the 65xx family of processors. The earlier Apple I was only available as a build-it-yourself kit.

## AppleScript

A scripting language for Mac OS computers.

## applet

An applet differs from an application in that is not meant to be run stand-alone but rather with the assistance of another program, usually a browser.

## AppleTalk

AppleTalk is a protocol for computer networks. It is arguably inferior to TCP/IP.

## Aqua

The default window manager for Mac OS X.

## Archie

Archie is a system for searching through FTP archives for particular files. It tends not to be used too much anymore as more general modern search engines are significantly more capable.

## ARM

An ARM is a RISC processor invented by Advanced RISC Machines, currently owned by Intel, and currently produced by both the above and Digital/Compaq. ARMs are different from most other processors in that they were not designed to maximize speed but rather to maximize speed per power consumed. Thus ARMs find most of their use on hand-held machines and PDAs. A few different OSes run on ARM based machines including Newton OS, JavaOS, and (soon) Windows CE and Linux. The StrongARM is a more recent design of the original ARM, and it is both faster and more power efficient than the original.

## ASCII

The ASCII character set is the most popular one in common use. People will often refer to a bare text file without complicated embedded format instructions as an ASCII file, and such files can usually be transferred from one computer system to another with relative ease. Unfortunately there are a few minor variations of it that pop up here and there, and if you receive a text file that seems subtly messed up with punctuation marks altered or upper and lower case reversed, you are probably encountering one of the ASCII variants. It is usually fairly straightforward to translate from one ASCII variant to another, though. The ASCII character set is seven bit while pure binary is usually eight bit, so transferring a binary file through ASCII channels will result in corruption and loss of data. Note also that the ASCII character set is a subset of the Unicode character set.

## ASK

A protocol for an infrared communications port on a device. It predates the IrDA compliant infrared communications protocol and is not compatible with it. Many devices with infrared communications support both, but some only support one or the other.

## assembly language

Assembly language is essentially machine language that has had some of the numbers replaced by somewhat easier to remember mnemonics in an attempt to make it more human-readable. The program that converts assembly language to machine language is called an assembler. While assembly language predates FORTRAN, it is not typically what people think of when they discuss computer languages.

## Atom

Atom is an intended replacement for RSS and like it is used for syndicating a web site's content. It is currently not nearly as popular or well-supported by software applications, however.

## authoring system

Any GUIs method of designing new software can be called an authoring system. Any computer language name with the word "visual" in front of it is probably a version of that language built with some authoring system capabilities. It appears that the first serious effort to produce a commercial quality authoring system took place in the mid eighties for the Amiga.

## AWK

AWK is an interpreted language developed in 1977 by Aho, Weinberger, & Kernighan. It gets its name from its creators' initials. It is not particularly fast, but it was designed for creating small throwaway programs rather than full-blown applications -- it is designed to make the writing of the program fast, not the program itself. It is quite portable with versions existing for numerous platforms, including a free GNU version. Plus, virtually every version of UNIX in the world comes with AWK built-in.

## BASIC

The **B**eginners' **A**ll-purpose **S**ymbolic **I**nstruction **C**ode is a computer language developed by Kemeny & Kurtz in 1964. Although it is traditionally interpreted, compilers exist for many platforms. While the interpreted form is typically fairly slow, the compiled form is often quite fast, usually faster than Pascal. The biggest problem with BASIC is portability; versions for different machines are often completely unlike each other; Amiga BASIC at first glance looks more like Pascal, for example. Portability problems actually go beyond even the cross platform level; in fact, most machines have multiple versions of incompatible BASICs available for use. The most popular version of BASIC today is called Visual BASIC. Like all BASICs it has portability issues, but it has some of the advantages of an authoring system so it is relatively easy to use.

## baud

A measure of communications speed, used typically for modems indicating how many bits per second can be transmitted.

## BBS

A **b**ulletin **b**oard **s**ystem is a computer that can be directly connected to via modem and provides various services like e-mail, chatting, newsgroups, and file downloading. BBSs have waned in popularity as more and more people are instead connecting to the Internet, but they are still used for product support and local area access. Most current BBSs provide some sort of gateway connection to the Internet.

## bcode

Identical in intent to uucode, bcode is slightly more efficient and more portable across different computer types. It is the preferred method used by MIME.

## BeOS

A lightweight OS available for both PowerPC and x86 based machines. It is often referred to simply as "Be".

**beta**

A beta version of something is not yet ready for prime time but still possibly useful to related developers and other interested parties. Expect beta software to crash more than properly released software does. Traditionally beta versions (of commercial software) are distributed only to selected testers who are often then given a discount on the proper version after its release in exchange for their testing work. Beta versions of non-commercial software are more often freely available to anyone who has an interest.

**binary**

There are two meanings for binary in common computer usage. The first is the name of the number system in which there are only zeros and ones. This is important to computers because all computer data is ultimately a series of zeros and ones, and thus can be represented by binary numbers. The second is an offshoot of the first; data that is not meant to be intepreted through a common character set (like ASCII) is typically referred to as binary data. Pure binary data is typically eight bit data, and transferring a binary file through ASCII channels without prior modification will result in corruption and loss of data. Binary data can be turned into ASCII data via uucoding or bcoding.

**bit**

A bit can either be on or off; one or zero. All computer data can ultimately be reduced to a series of bits. The term is also used as a (very rough) measure of sound quality, color quality, and even procesor capability by considering the fact that series of bits can represent binary numbers. For example (without getting too technical), an eight bit image can contain at most 256 distinct colors while a sixteen bit image can contain at most 65,536 distinct colors.

**bitmap**

A bitmap is a simplistic representation of an image on a computer, simply indicating whether or not pixels are on or off, and sometimes indicating their color. Often fonts are represented as bitmaps. The term "pixmap" is sometimes used similarly; typically when a distinction is made, pixmap refers to color images and bitmap refers to monochrome images.

**blog**

Short for web log, a blog (or weblog, or less commonly, 'blog) is a web site containing periodic (usually frequent) posts. Blogs are usually syndicated via either some type of RSS or Atom and often supports TrackBacks. It is not uncommon for blogs to function much like newspaper columns. A blogger is someone who writes for and maintains a blog.

**boolean**

Boolean algebra is the mathematics of base two numbers. Since base two numbers have only two values, zero and one, there is a good analogy between base two numbers and the logical values "true" & "false". In common usage, booleans are therefore considered to be simple logical values like true & false and the operations that relate them, most typically "and", "or" and "not". Since everyone has a basic understanding of the concepts of true & false and basic conjunctions, everyone also has a basic understanding of boolean concepts -- they just may not realize it.

**byte**

A byte is a grouping of bits. It is typically eight bits, but there are those who use non-standard byte sizes. Bytes are usually measured in large groups, and the term "kilobyte" (often abbreviated as K) means one-thousand twenty-four (1024) bytes; the term "megabyte" (often abbreviated as M) means one-thousand twenty-four (1024) K; the term gigabyte (often abbreviated as G) means one-thousand twenty-four (1024) M; and the term "terabyte" (often abbreviated as T) means one-thousand twenty-four (1024) G. Memory is typically measured in kilobytes or megabytes, and disk space is typically measured in megabytes or gigabytes. Note that the multipliers here are 1024 instead of the more common 1000 as would be used in the metric system. This is to make it easier to work with the binary number system. Note also that some hardware manufacturers will use the smaller 1000 multiplier on M & G quantities to make their disk drives seem larger than they really are; buyer beware.

**bytecode**

Sometimes computer languages that are said to be either interpreted or compiled are in fact neither and are more accurately said to be somewhere in between. Such languages are compiled into bytecode which is then interpreted on the target system. Bytecode tends to be binary but will work on any machine with the appropriate runtime environment (or virtual machine) for it.

**C**

C is one of the most popular computer languages in the world, and quite possibly *the* most popular. It is a compiled langauge widely supported on many platforms. It tends to be more portable than FORTRAN but less portable than Java; it has been standardized by ANSI as "ANSI C" -- older versions are called either "K&R C" or "Kernighan and Ritchie C" (in honor of C's creators), or sometimes just "classic C". Fast and simple, it can be applied to all manner of general purpose tasks. C compilers are made by several companies, but the free GNU version (gcc) is still considered one of the best. Newer C-like object-oriented languages include both Java and C++.

**C#**

C# is a compiled object-oriented language based heavily on C++ with some Java features.

**C++**

C++ is a compiled object-oriented language. Based heavily on C, C++ is nearly as fast and can often be thought of as being just C with added features. It is currently probably the second most popular object-oriented language, but it has the drawback of being fairly complex -- the much simpler but somewhat slower Java is probably the most popular object-oriented language. Note that C++ was developed independently of the somewhat similar Objective-C; it is however related to Objective-C++.

**C64/128**

The Commodore 64 computer to this day holds the record for being the most successful model of computer ever made with even the lowest estimates being in the tens of millions. Its big brother, the Commodore 128, was not quite as popular but still sold several million units. Both units sported ROM-based BASIC and used it as a default "OS". The C128 also came with CP/M (it was a not-often-exercized option on the C64). In their later days they were also packaged with GEOS. Both are based on 65xx family processors. They are still in use today and boast a friendly and surprisingly active user community. There is even a current effort to port Linux to the C64 and C128 machines.

**CDE**

The **c**ommon **d**esktop **e**nvironment is a popular commercial window manager (and much more -- as its name touts, it is more of a desktop environment) that runs under X-Windows. Free work-alike versions are also available.

**chain**

Some computer devices support chaining, the ability to string multiple devices in a sequence plugged into just one computer port. Often, but not always, such a chain will require some sort of terminator to mark the end. For an example, a SCSI scanner may be plugged into a SCSI CD-ROM drive that is plugged into a SCSI hard drive that is in turn plugged into the main computer. For all these components to work properly, the scanner would also have to have a proper terminator in use. Device chaining has been around a long time, and it is interesting to note that C64/128 serial devices supported it from the very beginning. Today the most common low-cost chainable devices in use support USB while the fastest low-cost chainable devices in use support FireWire.

**character set**

Since in reality all a computer can store are series of zeros and ones, representing common things like text takes a little work. The solution is to view the series of zeros and ones instead as a sequence of bytes, and map each one to a particular letter, number, or symbol. The full mapping is called a character set. The most popular character set is commonly referred to as ASCII. The second most popular character set these days is Unicode (and it will probably eventually surpass ASCII). Other fairly common character sets include EBCDIC and PETSCII. They are generally quite different from one another; programs exist to convert between them on most platforms, though. Usually EBCDIC is only found on really old machines.

**CISC**

**C**omplex **i**nstruction **s**et **c**omputing is one of the two main types of processor design in use today. It is slowly losing popularity to RISC designs; currently all the fastest processors in the world are RISC. The most popular current CISC processor is the x86, but there are also still some 68xx, 65xx, and Z80s in use.

**CLI**

A command-line interface is a text-based means of communicating with a program, especially an OS. This is the sort of interface used by MS-DOS, or a UNIX shell window.

**COBOL**

The **Co**mmon **B**usiness **O**riented **L**anguage is a language developed back in 1959 and still used by some businesses. While it is relatively portable, it is still disliked by many professional programmers simply because COBOL programs tend to be physically longer than equivalent programs written in almost any other language in common use.

**compiled**

If a program is compiled, its original human-readable source has been converted into a form more easily used by a computer prior to it being run. Such programs will generally run more quickly than interpreted programs, because time was pre-spent in the compilation phase. A program that compiles other programs is called a compiler.

**compression**

It is often possible to remove redundant information or capitalize on patterns in data to make a file smaller. Usually when a file has been compressed, it cannot be used until it is uncompressed. Image files are common exceptions, though, as many popular image file formats have compression built-in.

**cookie**

A cookie is a small file that a web page on another machine writes to your personal machine's disk to store various bits of information. Many people strongly detest cookies and the whole idea of them, and most browsers allow the reception of cookies to be disabled or at least selectively disabled, but it should be noted that both Netscape and MSIE have silent cookie reception enabled by default. Sites that maintain shopping carts or remember a reader's last position have legitimate uses for cookies. Sites without such functionality that still spew cookies with distant (or worse, non-existent) expiration dates should perhaps be treated with a little caution.

**CP/M**

An early DOS for desktops, CP/M runs on both Z80 and the x86 based machines. CP/M provides only a CLI and there really is not any standard way to get a window manager to run on top of it. It is fairly complex and tricky to use. In spite of all this, CP/M was once the most popular DOS and is still in use today.

**crash**

If a bug in a program is severe enough, it can cause that program to crash, or to become inoperable without being restarted. On machines that are not multitasking, the entire machine will crash and have to be rebooted. On machines that are only partially multitasking the entire machine will sometimes crash and have to be rebooted. On machines that are fully multitasking, the machine should never crash and require a reboot.

**Cray**

A Cray is a high-end computer used for research and frequently heavy-duty graphics applications. Modern Crays typically have Solaris for their OS and sport sixty-four RISC processors; older ones had various other configurations. Current top-of-the-line Crays can have over 2000 processors.

**crippleware**
Crippleware is a variant of shareware that will either self-destruct after its trial period or has built-in limitations to its functionality that get removed after its purchase.

**CSS**
Cascading style sheets are used in conjunction with HTML and XHTML to define the layout of web pages. While CSS is how current web pages declare how they should be displayed, it tends not to be supported well (if at all) by ancient browsers. XSL performs this same function more generally.

**desktop publisher**
A program for creating newspapers, magazines, books, etc. Some common desktop publishing programs include FrameMaker, PageMaker, InDesign, and GeoPublish.

**DHTML**
Dynamic HTML is simply the combined use of both CSS and JavaScript together in the same document; a more extreme form is called AJaX. Note that DHTML is quite different from the similarly named DTML.

**dict**
A protocol used for looking up definitions across a network (in particular the Internet).

**digital camera**
A digital camera looks and behaves like a regular camera, except instead of using film, it stores the image it sees in memory as a file for later transfer to a computer. Many digital cameras offer additional storage besides their own internal memory; a few sport some sort of disk but the majority utilize some sort of flash card. Digital cameras currently lack the resolution and color palette of real cameras, but are usually much more convenient for computer applications. Another related device is called a scanner.

**DIMM**
A physical component used to add RAM to a computer. Similar to, but incompatible with, SIMMs.

**DNS**
Domain name service is the means by which a name (like www.saugus.net or ftp.saugus.net) gets converted into a real Internet address that points to a particular machine.

**DoS**
In a denial of service attack, many individual (usually compromised) computers are used to try and simultaneously access the same public resource with the intent of overburdening it so that it will not be able to adequately serve its normal users.

**DOS**
A disk operating system manages disks and other system resources. Sort of a subset of OSes, sort of an archaic term for the same. MS-DOS is the most popular program currently calling itself a DOS. CP/M was the most popular prior to MS-DOS.

**download**
To download a file is to copy it from a remote computer to your own. The opposite is upload.

**DR-DOS**
The DOS currently produced by Caldera (originally produced by Design Research as a successor to CP/M) designed to work like MS-DOS. While similar to CP/M in many ways, it utilizes simpler commands. It provides only a CLI, but either Windows 3.1 or GEOS may be run on top of it to provide a GUI. It only runs on x86 based machines.

**driver**
A driver is a piece of software that works with the OS to control a particular piece of hardware, like a printer or a scanner or a mouse or whatever.

**DRM**

Depending upon whom you ask, DRM can stand for either Digital Rights Management or Digital Restrictions Management. In either case, DRM is used to place restrictions upon the usage of digital media ranging from software to music to video.

**DTML**

The **D**ocument **T**emplate **M**ark-up **L**anguage is a subset of SGML and a superset of HTML used for creating documents that dynamically adapt to external conditions using its own custom tags and a little bit of Python. Note that it is quite different from the similarly named DHTML.

**EDBIC**

The EDBIC character set is similar to (but less popular than) the ASCII character set in concept, but is significantly different in layout. It tends to be found only on old machines..

**emacs**

Emacs is both one of the most powerful and one of the most popular text editing programs in existence. Versions can be found for most platforms, and in fact multiple companies make versions, so for a given platform there might even be a choice. There is even a free GNU version available. The drawback with emacs is that it is not in the least bit lightweight. In fact, it goes so far in the other direction that even its advocates will occasionally joke about it. It is however extremely capable. Almost anything that one would need to relating to text can be done with emacs and is probably built-in. Even if one manages to find something that emacs was not built to do, emacs has a built-in Lisp interpreter capable of not only extending its text editing capabilities, but even of being used as a scripting language in its own right.

**embedded**

An embedded system is a computer that lives inside another device and acts as a component of that device. For example, current cars have an embedded computer under the hood that helps regulate much of their day to day operation.

An embedded file is a file that lives inside another and acts as a portion of that file. This is frequently seen with HTML files having embedded audio files; audio files often embedded in HTML include AU files, MIDI files, SID files, WAV files, AIFF files, and MOD files. Most browsers will ignore these files unless an appropriate plug-in is present.

**emulator**

An emulator is a program that allows one computer platform to mimic another for the purposes of running its software. Typically (but not always) running a program through an emulator will not be quite as pleasant an experience as running it on the real system.

**endian**

A processor will be either "big endian" or "little endian" based upon the manner in which it encodes multiple byte values. There is no difference in performance between the two encoding methods, but it is one of the sources of difficulty when reading binary data on different platforms.

**environment**

An environment (sometimes also called a runtime environment) is a collection of external variable items or parameters that a program can access when run. Information about the computer's hardware and the user can often be found in the environment.

**EPOC**

EPOC is a lightweight OS. It is most commonly found on the Psion PDA.

**extension**

Filename extensions originate back in the days of CP/M and basically allow a very rough grouping of different file types by putting a tag at the end of the name. To further complicate matters, the tag is sometimes separated by the name proper by a period "." and sometimes by a tab. While extensions are semi-enforced on CP/M, MS-DOS, and MS-Windows, they have no real meaning aside from convention on other platforms and are only optional.

**FAQ**

A frequently asked questions file attempts to provide answers for all commonly asked questions related to a given topic.

**FireWire**

An incredibly fast type of serial port that offers many of the best features of SCSI at a lower price. Faster than most types of parallel port, a single FireWire port is capable of chaining many devices without the need of a terminator. FireWire is similar in many respects to USB but is significantly faster and somewhat more expensive. It is heavily used for connecting audio/video devices to computers, but is also used for connecting storage devices like drives and other assorted devices like printers and scanners.

**fixed width**

As applied to a font, fixed width means that every character takes up the same amount of space. That is, an "i" will be just as wide as an "m" with empty space being used for padding. The opposite is variable width. The most common fixed width font is Courier.

**flash**

Flash memory is similar to RAM. It has one significant advantage: it does not lose its contents when power is lost; it has two main disadvantages: it is slower, and it eventually wears out. Flash memory is frequently found in PCMCIA cards.

**font**

In a simplistic sense, a font can be thought of as the physical description of a character set. While the character set will define what sets of bits map to what letters, numbers, and other symbols, the font will define what each letter, number, and other symbol looks like. Fonts can be either fixed width or variable width and independently, either bitmapped or vectored. The size of the large characters in a font is typically measured in points.

**Forth**

A language developed in 1970 by Moore. Forth is fairly portable and has versions on many different platforms. While it is no longer an very popular language, many of its ideas and concepts have been carried into other computer programs. In particular, some programs for doing heavy-duty mathematical and engineering work use Forth-like interfaces.

**FORTRAN**

FORTRAN stands for **formula translation** and is the oldest computer language in the world. It is typically compiled and is quite fast. Its primary drawbacks are portability and ease-of-use -- often different FORTRAN compilers on different platforms behave quite differently in spite of standardization efforts in 1966 (FORTRAN 66 or FORTRAN IV), 1978 (FORTRAN 77), and 1991 (FORTRAN 90). Today languages like C and Java are more popular, but FORTRAN is still heavily used in military software. It is somewhat amusing to note that when FORTRAN was first released back in 1958 its advocates thought that it would mean the end of software bugs. In truth of course by making the creation of more complex software practical, computer languages have merely created new types of software bugs.

**FreeBSD**

A free variant of Berkeley UNIX available for Alpha and x86 based machines. It is not as popular as Linux.

**freeware**

Freeware is software that is available for free with no strings attached. The quality is often superb as the authors are also generally users.

**FTP**

The **file transfer protocol** is one of the most commonly used methods of copying files across the Internet. It has its origins on UNIX machines, but has been adapted to almost every type of computer in existence and is built into many browsers. Most FTP programs have two modes of operation, ASCII, and binary. Transmitting an ASCII file via the ASCII mode of operation is more efficient and cleaner. Transmitting a binary file via the ASCII mode of operation will result in a broken binary file. Thus the FTP programs that do not support both modes of operation will typically only do the binary mode, as binary transfers are capable of transferring both kinds of data without corruption.

**gateway**

A gateway connects otherwise separate computer networks.

**GEOS**

The **g**raphic **e**nvironment **o**perating **s**ystem is a lightweight OS with a GUI. It runs on several different processors, including the 65xx (different versions for different machines -- there are versions for the C64, the C128, and the Apple ][, each utilizing the relevant custom chip sets), the x86 (although the x86 version is made to run on top of MS-DOS (or PC-DOS or DR-DOS) and is not strictly a full OS or a window manager, rather it is somewhat in between, like Windows 3.1) and numerous different PDAs, embedded devices, and hand-held machines. It was originally designed by Berkeley Softworks (no real relation to the Berkeley of UNIX fame) but is currently in a more interesting state: the company GeoWorks develops and promotes development of GEOS for hand-held devices, PDAs, & and embedded devices and owns (but has ceased further development on) the x86 version. The other versions are owned (and possibly still being developed) by the company CMD.

**GHz** & **gigahertz**

One gigahertz is equivalent to 1000 megahertz, or 1,000,000,000 hertz.

**Glulx**

A virtual machine optimized for running interactive fiction, interactive tutorials, and other interactive things of a primarily textual nature. Glulx has been ported to several platforms, and in in many ways an upgrade to the Z-machine.

**GNOME**

The **G**NU **n**etwork **o**bject **m**odel **e**nvironment is a popular free window manager (and much more -- as its name touts, it is more of a desktop environment) that runs under X-Windows. It is a part of the GNU project.

**GNU**

GNU stands for **G**NU's **n**ot **U**NIX and is thus a recursive acronym (and unlike the animal name, the "G" here is pronounced). At any rate, the GNU project is an effort by the Free Software Foundation (FSF) to make all of the traditional UNIX utilities free for whoever wants them. The Free Software Foundation programmers know their stuff, and the quality of the GNU software is on par with the best produced commercially, and often better. All of the GNU software can be downloaded for free or obtained on CD-ROM for a small service fee. Documentation for all GNU software can be downloaded for free or obtained in book form for a small service fee. The Free Software Foundation pays its bills from the collection of service fees and the sale of T-shirts, and exists mostly through volunteer effort. It is based in Cambridge, MA.

**gopher**

Though not as popular as FTP or http, the gopher protocol is implemented by many browsers and numerous other programs and allows the transfer of files across networks. In some respects it can be thought of as a hybrid between FTP and http, although it tends not to be as good at raw file transfer as FTP and is not as flexible as http. The collection of documents available through gopher is often called "gopherspace", and it should be noted that gopherspace is older than the web. It should also be noted that gopher is not getting as much attention as it once did, and surfing through gopherspace is a little like exploring a ghost town, but there is an interesting VR interface available for it, and some things in gopherspace still have not been copied onto the web.

**GUI**

A **g**raphical **u**ser **i**nterface is a graphics-based means of communicating with a program, especially an OS or window manager. In fact, a window manager can be thought of as a GUI for a CLI OS.

**HP-UX**

HP-UX is the version of UNIX designed by Hewlett-Packard to work with their PA-RISC and

68xx based machines.

## HTML

The **H**ypertext **M**ark-up **L**anguage is the language currently most frequently used to express web pages (although it is rapidly being replaced by XHTML). Every browser has the built-in ability to understand HTML. Some browsers can additionally understand Java and browse FTP areas. HTML is a proper subset of SGML.

## http

The **h**ypertext **t**ransfer **p**rotocol is the native protocol of browsers and is most typically used to transfer HTML formatted files. The secure version is called "https".

## Hurd

The Hurd is the official GNU OS. It is still in development and is not yet supported on too many different processors, but promises to be the most powerful OS available. It (like all the GNU software) is free.

## Hz & hertz

Hertz means cycles per second, and makes no assumptions about what is cycling. So, for example, if a fluorescent light flickers once per jiffy, it has a 60 Hz flicker. More typical for computers would be a program that runs once per jiffy and thus has a 60 Hz frequency, or larger units of hertz like kHz, MHz, GHz, or THz.

## i18n

Commonly used to abbreviate the word "internationalization". There are eighteen letters between the "i" and the "n". Similar to (and often used along with) i18n.

## iCalendar

The iCalendar standard refers to the format used to store calendar type information (including events, to-do items, and journal entries) on the Internet. iCalendar data can be found on some World-Wide-Web pages or attached to e-mail messages.

## icon

A small graphical display representing an object, action, or modifier of some sort.

## IDE

Loosely speaking, a disk format sometimes used by MS-Windows, Mac OS, AmigaOS, and (rarely) UNIX. EIDE is enhanced IDE; it is much faster. Generally IDE is inferior (but less expensive) to SCSI, but it varies somewhat with system load and the individual IDE and SCSI components themselves. The quick rundown is that: SCSI-I and SCSI-II will almost always outperform IDE; EIDE will almost always outperform SCSI-I and SCSI-II; SCSI-III and UltraSCSI will almost always outperform EIDE; and heavy system loads give an advantage to SCSI. Note that although loosely speaking it is just a format difference, it is deep down a hardware difference.

## Inform

A compiled, object-oriented language optimized for creating interactive fiction.

## infrared communications

A device with an infrared port can communicate with other devices at a distance by beaming infrared light signals. Two incompatible protocols are used for infrared communications: IrDA and ASK. Many devices support both.

## Instant Messenger

AOL's Instant Messenger is is a means of chatting over the Internet in real-time. It allows both open group discussions and private conversations. Instant Messenger uses a different, proprietary protocol from the more standard IRC, and is not supported on as many platforms.

## interactive fiction

Interactive fiction (often abbreviated "IF" or "I-F") is a form of literature unique to the computer. While the reader cannot influence the direction of a typical story, the reader plays a more active role in an interactive fiction story and completely controls its direction. Interactive fiction works come in all the sizes and genres available to standard fiction, and in fact are not always even fiction per se (interactive tutorials exist and are slowly becoming more common).

**interpreted**

If a program is interpreted, its actual human-readable source is read as it is run by the computer. This is generally a slower process than if the program being run has already been compiled.

**intranet**

An intranet is a private network. There are many intranets scattered all over the world. Some are connected to the Internet via gateways.

**IP**

IP is the family of protocols that makes up the Internet. The two most common flavors are TCP/IP and UDP/IP.

**IRC**

Internet relay chat is a means of chatting over the Internet in real-time. It allows both open group discussions and private conversations. IRC programs are provided by many different companies and will work on many different platforms. AOL's Instant Messenger utilizes a separate incompatible protocol but is otherwise very similar.

**IrDA**

The Infrared Data Association (IrDA) is a voluntary organization of various manufacturers working together to ensure that the infrared communications between different computers, PDAs, printers, digital cameras, remote controls, etc. are all compatible with each other regardless of brand. The term is also often used to designate an IrDA compliant infrared communications port on a device. Informally, a device able to communicate via IrDA compliant infrared is sometimes simply said to "have IrDA". There is also an earlier, incompatible, and usually slower type of infrared communications still in use called ASK.

**IRI**

An Internationalized Resource Identifier is just a URI with i18n.

**IRIX**

The variant of UNIX designed by Silicon Graphics, Inc. IRIX machines are known for their graphics capabilities and were initially optimized for multimedia applications.

**ISDN**

An integrated service digital network line can be simply looked at as a digital phone line. ISDN connections to the Internet can be four times faster than the fastest regular phone connection, and because it is a digital connection a modem is not needed. Any computer hooked up to ISDN will typically require other special equipment in lieu of the modem, however. Also, both phone companies and ISPs charge more for ISDN connections than regular modem connections.

**ISP**

An Internet service provider is a company that provides Internet support for other entities. AOL (America Online) is a well-known ISP.

**Java**

A computer language designed to be both fairly lightweight and extremely portable. It is tightly bound to the web as it is the primary language for web applets. There has also been an OS based on Java for use on small hand-held, embedded, and network computers. It is called JavaOS. Java can be either interpreted or compiled. For web applet use it is almost always interpreted. While its interpreted form tends not to be very fast, its compiled form can often rival languages like C++ for speed. It is important to note however that speed is not Java's primary purpose -- raw speed is considered secondary to portabilty and ease of use.

**JavaScript**

JavaScript (in spite of its name) has nothing whatsoever to do with Java (in fact, it's arguably more like Newton Script than Java). JavaScript is an interpreted language built into a browser to provide a relatively simple means of adding interactivity to web pages. It is only supported on a few different browsers, and tends not to work exactly the same on different versions. Thus its use on the Internet is somewhat restricted to fairly simple programs. On intranets where there are usually fewer browser versions in use, JavaScript has been used to implement much more complex and impressive programs.

### jiffy

A jiffy is 1/60 of a second. Jiffies are to seconds as seconds are to minutes.

### joystick

A joystick is a physical device typically used to control objects on a computer screen. It is frequently used for games and sometimes used in place of a mouse.

### JSON

The JSON is used for data interchange between programs, an area in which the ubiquitous XML is not too well-suited. JSON is lightweight and works extremely cleanly with languages languages including JavaScript, Python, Java, C++, and many others.

### JSON-RPC

JSON-RPC is like XML-RPC but is significantly more lightweight since it uses JSON in lieu of XML.

### KDE

The K desktop environment is a popular free window manager (and much more -- as its name touts, it is more of a desktop environment) that runs under X-Windows.

### Kerberos

Kerberos is a network authentication protocol. Basically it preserves the integrity of passwords in any untrusted network (like the Internet). Kerberized applications work hand-in-hand with sites that support Kerberos to ensure that passwords cannot be stolen.

### kernel

The very heart of an OS is often called its kernel. It will usually (at minimum) provide some libraries that give programmers access to its various features.

### kHz & kilohertz

One kilohertz is equivalent to 1000 hertz. Some older computers have clock speeds measured in kHz.

### l10n

Commonly used to abbreviate the word "localization". There are ten letters between the "l" and the "n". Similar to (and often used along with) i18n.

### LDAP

The Lightweight Directory Access Protocol provides a means of sharing address book type of information across an intranet or even across the Internet. Note too that "address book type of information" here is pretty broad; it often includes not just human addresses, but machine addresses, printer configurations, and similar.

### library

A selection of routines used by programmers to make computers do particular things.

### lightweight

Something that is lightweight will not consume computer resources (such as RAM and disk space) too much and will thus run on less expensive computer systems.

### Linux

Believe it or not, one of the fastest, most robust, and powerful multitasking OSes is available for free. Linux can be downloaded for free or be purchased on CD-ROM for a small service charge. A handful of companies distribute Linux including Red Hat, Debian, Caldera, and many others. Linux is also possibly available for more hardware combinations than any other OS (with the possible exception of NetBSD. Supported processors include: Alpha, PowerPC, SPARC, x86, and 68xx. Most processors currently not supported are currently works-in-progress or even available in beta. For example, work is currently underway to provide support for PA-RISC, 65xx, StrongARM, and Z80. People have even successfully gotten Linux working on PDAs. As you may have guessed, Linux can be made quite lightweight. Linux is a variant of UNIX and as such, most of the traditional UNIX software will run on Linux. This especially includes the GNU software, most of which comes with the majority of Linux distributions. Fast, reliable, stable, and inexpensive, Linux is popular with ISPs, software developers, and home hobbyists alike.

## Lisp

Lisp stands for **lis**t **p**rocessing and is the second oldest computer language in the world. Being developed in 1959, it lost the title to FORTRAN by only a few months. It is typically interpreted, but compilers are available for some platforms. Attempts were made to standardize the language, and the standard version is called "Common Lisp". There have also been efforts to simplify the language, and the results of these efforts is another language called Scheme. Lisp is a fairly portable language, but is not particularly fast. Today, Lisp is most widely used with AI software.

## load

There are two popular meanings for load. The first means to fetch some data or a program from a disk and store it in memory. The second indicates the amount of work a component (especially a processor) is being made to do.

## Logo

Logo is an interpreted language designed by Papert in 1966 to be a tool for helping people (especially kids) learn computer programming concepts. In addition to being used for that purpose, it is often used as a language for controlling mechanical robots and other similar devices. Logo interfaces even exist for building block / toy robot sets. Logo uses a special graphics cursor called "the turtle", and Logo is itself sometimes called "Turtle Graphics". Logo is quite portable but not particularly fast. Versions can be found on almost every computer platform in the world. Additionally, some other languages (notably some Pascal versions) provide Logo-like interfaces for graphics-intensive programming.

## lossy

If a process is lossy, it means that a little quality is lost when it is performed. If a format is lossy, it means that putting data into that format (or possibly even manipulating it in that format) will cause some slight loss. Lossy processes and formats are typically used for performance or resource utilization reasons. The opposite of lossy is lossless.

## Lua

Lua is a simple interpreted language. It is extremely portable, and free versions exist for most platforms.

## Mac OS

Mac OS is the OS used on Macintosh computers. There are two distinctively different versions of it; everything prior to version 10 (sometimes called Mac OS Classic) and everything version 10 or later (called Mac OS X).

## Mac OS Classic

The OS created by Apple and originally used by Macs is frequently (albeit slightly incorrectly) referred to as Mac OS Classic (officially Mac OS Classic is this original OS running under the modern Mac OS X in emulation. Mac OS combines the functionality of both an OS and a window manager and is often considered to be the easiest OS to use. It is partially multitasking but will still sometimes crash when dealing with a buggy program. It is probably the second most popular OS, next only to Windows 'XP (although it is quickly losing ground to Mac OS X) and has excellent driver support and boasts a fair selection of games. Mac OS will run on PowerPC and 68xx based machines.

## Mac OS X

Mac OS X (originally called Rhapsody) is the industrial strength OS produced by Apple to run on both PowerPC and x86 systems (replacing what is often referred to as Mac OS Classic. Mac OS X is at its heart a variant of UNIX and possesses its underlying power (and the ability to run many of the traditional UNIX tools, including the GNU tools). It also was designed to mimic other OSes on demand via what it originally refered to as "boxes" (actually high-performance emulators); it has the built-in capability to run programs written for older Mac OS (via its "BlueBox", officially called Mac OS Classic) and work was started on making it also run Windows '95 / '98 / ME software (via what was called its "YellowBox"). There are also a few rumors going around that future versions may even be able to run Newton software (via the "GreenBox"). It provides a selection of two window managers built-in: Aqua and X-Windows (with Aqua being the default).

**machine language**

Machine language consists of the raw numbers that can be directly understood by a particular processor. Each processor's machine language will be different from other processors' machine language. Although called "machine language", it is not usually what people think of when talking about computer languages. Machine language dressed up with mnemonics to make it a bit more human-readable is called assembly language.

**Macintosh**

A Macintosh (or a Mac for short) is a computer system that has Mac OS for its OS. There are a few different companies that have produced Macs, but by far the largest is Apple. The oldest Macs are based on the 68xx processor; somewhat more recent Macs on the PowerPC processor, and current Macs on the x86 processor. The Macintosh was really the first general purpose computer to employ a GUI.

**MacTel**

An x86 based system running some flavor of Mac OS.

**mainframe**

A mainframe is any computer larger than a small piece of furniture. A modern mainframe is more powerful than a modern workstation, but more expensive and more difficult to maintain.

**MathML**

The **Math M**ark-up **L**anguage is a subset of XML used to represent mathematical formulae and equations. Typically it is found embedded within XHTML documents, although as of this writing not all popular browsers support it.

**megahertz**

A million cycles per second, abbreviated MHz. This is often used misleadingly to indicate processor speed, because while one might expect that a higher number would indicate a faster processor, that logic only holds true within a given type of processors as different types of processors are capable of doing different amounts of work within a cycle. For a current example, either a 200 MHz PowerPC or a 270 MHz SPARC will outperform a 300 MHz Pentium.

**Merced**

The Merced is a RISC processor developed by Intel with help from Hewlett-Packard and possibly Sun. It is just starting to be released, but is intended to eventually replace both the x86 and PA-RISC processors. Curiously, HP is recommending that everyone hold off using the first release and instead wait for the second one. It is expected some day to be roughly as fast as an Alpha or PowerPC. It is expected to be supported by future versions of Solaris, Windows-NT, HP-UX, Mac OS X, and Linux. The current semi-available Merced processor is called the Itanium. Its overall schedule is way behind, and some analysts predict that it never will really be released in significant quanitities.

**MFM**

Loosely speaking, An old disk format sometimes used by CP/M, MS-DOS, and MS-Windows. No longer too common as it cannot deliver close to the performance of either SCSI or IDE.

**middleware**

Software designed to sit in between an OS and applications. Common examples are Java and Tcl/Tk.

**MIME**

The **m**ulti-purpose **I**nternet **m**ail **e**xtensions specification describes a means of sending non-

ASCII data (such as images, sounds, foreign symbols, etc.) through e-mail. It commonly utilizes bcode.

## MMX

Multimedia extensions were built into some x86 CPUs to provide better performance for certain operations, most notably graphics and sound. It is similar to AltiVec on the PowerPC CPUs. Like AltiVec, it requires special software for full performance benefits to be realized.

## MOB

A **mo**vable **obj**ect is a graphical object that is manipulated separately from the background. These are seen all the time in computer games. When implemented in hardware, MOBs are sometimes called sprites.

## Modula-2 & Modula-3

Modula-2 is a procedural language based on Pascal by its original author in around the 1977 - 1979 time period. Modula-3 is an intended successor that adds support for object-oriented constructs (among other things). Modula-2 can be either compiled or interpreted, while Modula-3 tends to be just a compiled language.

## MOTD

A **m**essage **o**f **t**he **d**ay. Many computers (particularly more capable ones) are configured to display a MOTD when accessed remotely.

## Motif

Motif is a popular commercial window manager that runs under X-Windows. Free work-alike versions are also available.

## MS-DOS

The DOS produced by Microsoft. Early versions of it bear striking similarities to the earlier CP/M, but it utilizes simpler commands. It provides only a CLI, but either OS/2, Windows 3.1, Windows '95, Windows '98, Windows ME, or GEOS may be run on top of it to provide a GUI. It only runs on x86 based machines.

## MS-Windows

MS-Windows is the name collectively given to several somewhat incompatible OSes all produced by Microsoft. They are: Windows CE, Windows NT, Windows 3.1, Windows '95, Windows '98, Windows ME, Windows 2000, and Windows XP.

## MUD

A **m**ulti-**u**ser **d**imension (also sometimes called multi-user dungeon, but in either case abbreviated to "MUD") is sort of a combination between the online chatting abilities provided by something like IRC and a role-playing game. A MUD built with object oriented principles in mind is called a "Multi-user dimension object-oriented", or MOO. Yet another variant is called a "multi-user shell", or MUSH. Still other variants are called multi-user role-playing environments (MURPE) and multi-user environments (MUSE). There are probably more. In all cases the differences will be mostly academic to the regular user, as the same software is used to connect to all of them. Software to connect to MUDs can be found for most platforms, and there are even Java based ones that can run from within a browser.

## multitasking

Some OSes have built into them the ability to do several things at once. This is called multitasking, and has been in use since the late sixties / early seventies. Since this ability is built into the software, the overall system will be slower running two things at once than it will be running just one thing. A system may have more than one processor built into it though, and such a system will be capable of running multiple things at once with less of a performance hit.

## nagware

Nagware is a variant of shareware that will frequently remind its users to register.

## NetBSD

A free variant of Berkeley UNIX available for Alpha, x86, 68xx, PA-RISC, SPARC, PowerPC, ARM, and many other types of machines. Its emphasis is on portability.

**netiquette**

The established conventions of online politeness are called netiquette. Some conventions vary from site to site or online medium to online medium; others are pretty standard everywhere. Newbies are often unfamiliar with the conventional rules of netiquette and sometimes embarrass themselves accordingly. Be sure not to send that incredibly important e-mail message before reading about netiquette.

**newbie**

A newbie is a novice to the online world or computers in general.

**news**

Usenet news can generally be thought of as public e-mail as that is generally the way it behaves. In reality, it is implemented by different software and is often accessed by different programs. Different newsgroups adhere to different topics, and some are "moderated", meaning that humans will try to manually remove off-topic posts, especially spam. Most established newsgroups have a FAQ, and people are strongly encouraged to read the FAQ prior to posting.

**Newton**

Although Newton is officially the name of the lightweight OS developed by Apple to run on its MessagePad line of PDAs, it is often used to mean the MessagePads (and compatible PDAs) themselves and thus the term "Newton OS" is often used for clarity. The Newton OS is remarkably powerful; it is fully multitasking in spite of the fact that it was designed for small machines. It is optimized for hand-held use, but will readily transfer data to all manner of desktop machines. Historically it was the first PDA. Recently Apple announced that it will discontinue further development of the Newton platform, but will instead work to base future hand-held devices on either Mac OS or Mac OS X with some effort dedicated to making the new devices capable of running current Newton programs.

**Newton book**

Newton books provide all the functionality of ordinary books but add searching and hypertext capabilities. The format was invented for the Newton to provide a means of making volumes of data portable, and is particularly popular in the medical community as most medical references are available as Newton books and carrying around a one pound Newton is preferable to carrying around twenty pounds of books, especially when it comes to looking up something. In addition to medical books, numerous references, most of the classics, and many contemporary works of fiction are available as Newton books. Most fiction is available for free, most references cost money. Newton books are somewhat more capable than the similar Palm DOC; both are specific types of e-books.

**Newton Script**

A intepreted, object-oriented language for Newton MessagePad computers.

**nybble**

A nybble is half a byte, or four bits. It is a case of computer whimsy; it only stands to reason that a small byte should be called a nybble. Some authors spell it with an "i" instead of the "y", but the "y" is the original form.

**object-oriented**

While the specifics are well beyond the scope of this document, the term "object-oriented" applies to a philosophy of software creation. Often this philosophy is referred to as object-oriented design (sometimes abbreviated as OOD), and programs written with it in mind are referred to as object-oriented programs (often abbreviated OOP). Programming languages designed to help facilitate it are called object-oriented languages (sometimes abbreviated as OOL) and databases built with it in mind are called object-oriented databases (sometimes abbreviated as OODB or less fortunately OOD). The general notion is that an object-oriented approach to creating software starts with modeling the real-world problems trying to be solved in familiar real-world ways, and carries the analogy all the way down to structure of the program. This is of course a great over-simplification. Numerous object-oriented programming languages exist including: Java, C++, Modula-2, Newton Script, and ADA.

## Objective-C & ObjC

Objective-C (often called "ObjC" for short) is a compiled object-oriented language. Based heavily on C, Objective-C is nearly as fast and can often be thought of as being just C with added features. Note that it was developed independently of C++; its object-oriented extensions are more in the style of Smalltalk. It is however related to Objective-C++.

## Objective-C++ & ObjC++

Objective-C++ (often called "ObjC++" for short) is a curious hybrid of Objective-C and C++, allowing the syntax of both to coexist in the same source files.

## office suite

An office suite is a collection of programs including at minimum a word processor, spreadsheet, drawing program, and minimal database program. Some common office suites include MS-Office, AppleWorks, ClarisWorks, GeoWorks, Applixware, Corel Office, and StarOffice.

## open source

Open source software goes one step beyond freeware. Not only does it provide the software for free, it provides the original source code used to create the software. Thus, curious users can poke around with it to see how it works, and advanced users can modify it to make it work better for them. By its nature, open souce software is pretty well immune to all types of computer virus.

## OpenBSD

A free variant of Berkeley UNIX available for Alpha, x86, 68xx, PA-RISC, SPARC, and PowerPC based machines. Its emphasis is on security.

## OpenDocument & ODF

OpenDocument (or ODF for short) is the suite of open, XML-based office suite application formats defined by the OASIS consortium. It defines a platform-neutral, non-proprietary way of storing documents.

## OpenGL

A low-level 3D graphics library with an emphasis on speed developed by SGI.

## OS/2

OS/2 is the OS designed by IBM to run on x86 based machines. It is semi-compatible with MS-Windows. IBM's more industrial strength OS is called AIX.

## PA-RISC

The PA-RISC is a RISC processor developed by Hewlett-Packard. It is currently produced only by HP. At the moment only one OS runs on PA-RISC based machines: HP-UX. There is an effort underway to port Linux to them, though.

## Palm DOC

Palm DOC files are quite similar to (but slightly less capable than) Newton books. They were designed for Palm Pilots but can now be read on a couple other platforms, too. They are a specific type of e-book.

## Palm Pilot

The Palm Pilot (also called both just Palm and just Pilot, officially now just Palm) is the most popular PDA currently in use. It is one of the least capable PDAs, but it is also one of the smallest and least expensive. While not as full featured as many of the other PDAs (such as the Newton) it performs what features it does have quite well and still remains truly pocket-sized.

## parallel

Loosely speaking, parallel implies a situation where multiple things can be done simultaneously, like having multiple check-out lines each serving people all at once. Parallel connections are by their nature more expensive than serial ones, but usually faster. Also, in a related use of the word, often multitasking computers are said to be capable of running multiple programs in parallel.

## partition

Sometimes due to hardware limitations, disks have to be divided into smaller pieces. These pieces are called partitions.

## Pascal

Named after the mathematician Blaise Pascal, Pascal is a language designed by Niklaus Wirth originally in 1968 (and heavily revised in 1972) mostly for purposes of education and training people how to write computer programs. It is a typically compiled language but is still usually slower than C or FORTRAN. Wirth also created a more powerful object-oriented Pascal-like language called Modula-2.

## PC-DOS

The DOS produced by IBM designed to work like MS-DOS. Early versions of it bear striking similarities to the earlier CP/M, but it utilizes simpler commands. It provides only a CLI, but either Windows 3.1 or GEOS may be run on top of it to provide a GUI. It only runs on x86 based machines.

## PCMCIA

The **P**ersonal **C**omputer **M**emory **C**ard **I**nternational **A**ssociation is a standards body that concern themselves with PC Card technology. Often the PC Cards themselves are referred to as "PCMCIA cards". Frequently flash memory can be found in PC card form.

## Perl

Perl is an interpreted language extremely popular for web applications.

## PET

The Commodore PET (**P**ersonal **E**lectronic **T**ransactor) is an early (circa 1977-1980, around the same time as the Apple][) home computer featuring a ROM-based BASIC developed by Microsoft which it uses as a default "OS". It is based on the 65xx family of processors and is the precursor to the VIC-20.

## PETSCII

The PETSCII character set gets its name from "**PET** ASCII; it is a variant of the ASCII character set originally developed for the Commodore PET that swaps the upper and lower case characters and adds over a hundred graphic characters in addition to other small changes. If you encounter some text that seems to have uppercase where lowercase is expected and vice-versa, it is probably a PETSCII file.

## PHP

Named with a recursive acronym (PHP: Hypertext Preprocessor), PHP provides a means of creating web pages that dynamically modify themselves on the fly.

## ping

Ping is a protocol designed to check across a network to see if a particular computer is "alive" or not. Computers that recognize the ping will report back their status. Computers that are down will not report back anything at all.

## pixel

The smallest distinct point on a computer display is called a pixel.

## plug-in

A plug-in is a piece of software designed not to run on its own but rather work in cooperation with a separate application to increase that application's abilities.

## point

There are two common meanings for this word. The first is in the geometric sense; a position in space without size. Of course as applied to computers it must take up some space in practise (even if not in theory) and it is thus sometimes synonomous with pixel. The other meaning is related most typically to fonts and regards size. The exact meaning of it in this sense will unfortunately vary somewhat from person to person, but will often mean 1/72 of an inch. Even when it does not exactly mean 1/72 of an inch, larger point sizes always indicate larger fonts.

## PowerPC

The PowerPC is a RISC processor developed in a collaborative effort between IBM, Apple, and Motorola. It is currently produced by a few different companies, of course including its original developers. A few different OSes run on PowerPC based machines, including Mac OS, AIX, Solaris, Windows NT, Linux, Mac OS X, BeOS, and AmigaOS. At any given time, the fastest processor in the world is usually either a PowerPC or an Alpha, but sometimes SPARCs and PA-RISCs make the list, too.

**proprietary**

This simply means to be supplied by only one vendor. It is commonly misused. Currently, most processors are non-proprietary, some systems are non-proprietary, and every OS (except for arguably Linux) is proprietary.

**protocol**

A protocol is a means of communication used between computers. As long as both computers recognize the same protocol, they can communicate without too much difficulty over the same network or even via a simple direct modem connection regardless whether or not they are themselves of the same type. This means that WinTel boxes, Macs, Amigas, UNIX machines, etc., can all talk with one another provided they agree on a common protocol first.

**Psion**

The Psion is a fairly popular brand of PDA. Generally, it is in between a Palm and a Newton in capability. It runs the EPOC OS.

**Python**

Python is an interpreted, object-oriented language popular for Internet applications. It is extremely portable with free versions existing for virtually every platform.

**queue**

A queue is a waiting list of things to be processed. Many computers provide printing queues, for example. If something is being printed and the user requests that another item be printed, the second item will sit in the printer queue until the first item finishes printing at which point it will be removed from the queue and get printed itself.

**QuickDraw**

A high-level 3D graphics library with an emphasis on quick development time created by Apple.

**RAM**

Random access memory is the short-term memory of a computer. Any information stored in RAM will be lost if power goes out, but the computer can read from RAM far more quickly than from a drive.

**random access**

Also called "dynamic access" this indicates that data can be selected without having to skip over earlier data first. This is the way that a CD, record, laserdisc, or DVD will behave -- it is easy to selectively play a particular track without having to fast forward through earlier tracks. The other common behavior is called sequential access.

**RDF**

The Resource Description Framework is built upon an XML base and provides a more modern means of accessing data from Internet resources. It can provide metadata (including annotations) for web pages making (among other things) searching more capable. It is also being used to refashion some existing formats like RSS and iCalendar; in the former case it is already in place (at least for newer RSS versions), but it is still experimental in the latter case.

**real-time**

Something that happens in real-time will keep up with the events around it and never give any sort of "please wait" message.

**Rexx**

The Restructured Extended Executor is an interpreted language designed primarily to be embedded in other applications in order to make them consistently programmable, but also to be easy to learn and understand.

**RISC**

Reduced instruction set computing is one of the two main types of processor design in use today, the other being CISC. The fastest processors in the world today are all RISC designs. There are several popular RISC processors, including Alphas, ARMs, PA-RISCs, PowerPCs, and SPARCs.

### robot

A robot (or 'bot for short) in the computer sense is a program designed to automate some task, often just sending messages or collecting information. A spider is a type of robot designed to traverse the web performing some task (usually collecting data).

### robust

The adjective robust is used to describe programs that are better designed, have fewer bugs, and are less likely to crash.

### ROM

Read-only memory is similar to RAM only cannot be altered and does not lose its contents when power is removed.

### RSS

RSS stands for either Rich Site Summary, Really Simple Syndication, or RDF Site Summary, depending upon whom you ask. The general idea is that it can provide brief summaries of articles that appear in full on a web site. It is well-formed XML, and newer versions are even more specifically well-formed RDF.

### Ruby

Ruby is an interpreted, object-oriented language. Ruby was fairly heavily influenced by Perl, so people familiar with that language can typically transition to Ruby easily.

### scanner

A scanner is a piece of hardware that will examine a picture and produce a computer file that represents what it sees. A digital camera is a related device. Each has its own limitations.

### Scheme

Scheme is a typically interpreted computer language. It was created in 1975 in an attempt to make Lisp simpler and more consistent. Scheme is a fairly portable language, but is not particularly fast.

### script

A script is a series of OS commands. The term "batch file" means much the same thing, but is a bit dated. Typically the same sort of situations in which one would say DOS instead of OS, it would also be appropriate to say batch file instead of script. Scripts can be run like programs, but tend to perform simpler tasks. When a script is run, it is always interpreted.

### SCSI

Loosely speaking, a disk format sometimes used by MS-Windows, Mac OS, AmigaOS, and (almost always) UNIX. Generally SCSI is superior (but more expensive) to IDE, but it varies somewhat with system load and the individual SCSI and IDE components themselves. The quick rundown is that: SCSI-I and SCSI-II will almost always outperform IDE; EIDE will almost always outperform SCSI-I and SCSI-II; SCSI-III and UltraSCSI will almost always outperform EIDE; and heavy system loads give an advantage to SCSI. Note that although loosely speaking it is just a format difference, it is deep down a hardware difference.

### sequential access

This indicates that data cannot be selected without having to skip over earlier data first. This is the way that a cassette or video tape will behave. The other common behavior is called random access.

### serial

Loosely speaking, serial implies something that has to be done linearly, one at a time, like people being served in a single check-out line. Serial connections are by their nature less expensive than parallel connections (including things like SCSI) but are typically slower.

### server

A server is a computer designed to provide various services for an entire network. It is typically either a workstation or a mainframe because it will usually be expected to handle far greater loads than ordinary desktop systems. The load placed on servers also necessitates that they utilize robust OSes, as a crash on a system that is currently being used by many people is far worse than a crash on a system that is only being used by one person.

## SGML

The **S**tandard **G**eneralized **M**ark-up **L**anguage provides an extremely generalized level of mark-up. More common mark-up languages like HTML and XML are actually just popular subsets of SGML.

## shareware

Shareware is software made for profit that allows a trial period before purchase. Typically shareware can be freely downloaded, used for a period of weeks (or sometimes even months), and either purchased or discarded after it has been learned whether or not it will satisfy the user's needs.

## shell

A CLI designed to simplify complex OS commands. Some OSes (like AmigaOS, the Hurd, and UNIX) have built-in support to make the concurrent use of multiple shells easy. Common shells include the Korn Shell (ksh), the Bourne Shell (sh or bsh), the Bourne-Again Shell, (bash or bsh), the C-Shell (csh), etc.

## SIMM

A physical component used to add RAM to a computer. Similar to, but incompatible with, DIMMs.

## Smalltalk

Smalltalk is an efficient language for writing computer programs. Historically it is one of the first object-oriented languages, and is not only used today in its pure form but shows its influence in other languages like Objective-C.

## Solaris

Solaris is the commercial variant of UNIX currently produced by Sun. It is an industrial strength, nigh bulletproof, powerful multitasking OS that will run on SPARC, x86, and PowerPC based machines.

## spam

Generally spam is unwanted, unrequested e-mail or Usenet news. It is typically sent out in bulk to huge address lists that were automatically generated by various robots endlessly searching the Internet and newsgroups for things that resemble e-mail addresses. The legality of spam is a topic of much debate; it is at best only borderline legal, and spammers have been successfully persecuted in some states.

## SPARC

The SPARC is a RISC processor developed by Sun. The design was more or less released to the world, and it is currently produced by around a dozen different companies too numerous to even bother mentioning. It is worth noting that even computers made by Sun typically sport SPARCs made by other companies. A couple different OSes run on SPARC based machines, including Solaris, SunOS, and Linux. Some of the newer SPARC models are called UltraSPARCs.

## sprite

The term sprite originally referred to a small MOB, usually implemented in hardware. Lately it is also being used to refer to a single image used piecemeal within a Web site in order to avoid incurring the time penalty of downloading multiple files.

## SQL

SQL (pronounced **Sequel**) is an interpreted language specially designed for database access. It is supported by virtually every major modern database system.

## Sugar

The window manager used by the OLPC XO. It is made to run on top of Linux.

**SunOS**

SunOS is the commercial variant of UNIX formerly produced (but still supported) by Sun.

**SVG**

**S**calable **V**ector **G**raphics data is an XML file that is used to hold graphical data that can be resized without loss of quality. SVG data can be kept in its own file, or even embedded within a web page (although not all browsers are capable of displaying such data).

**Tcl/Tk**

The **T**ool **C**ommand **L**anguage is a portable interpreted computer language designed to be easy to use. Tk is a GUI toolkit for Tcl. Tcl is a fairly popular language for both integrating existing applications and for creating Web applets (note that applets written in Tcl are often called Tcklets). Tcl/Tk is available for free for most platforms, and plug-ins are available to enable many browsers to play Tcklets.

**TCP/IP**

TCP/IP is a protocol for computer networks. The Internet is largely built on top of TCP/IP (it is the more reliable of the two primary Internet Protocols -- TCP stands for **T**ransmission **C**ontrol **P**rotocol).

**terminator**

A terminator is a dedicated device used to mark the end of a device chain (as is most typically found with SCSI devices). If such a chain is not properly terminated, weird results can occur.

**TEX**

TEX (pronounced "tek") is a freely available, industrial strength typesetting program that can be run on many different platforms. These qualities make it exceptionally popular in schools, and frequently software developed at a university will have its documentation in TEX format. TEX is not limited to educational use, though; many professional books were typeset with TEX. TEX's primary drawback is that it can be quite difficult to set up initially.

**THz & terahertz**

One terahertz is equivalent to 1000 gigahertz.

**TrackBack**

TrackBacks essentially provide a means whereby different web sites can post messages to one another not just to inform each other about citations, but also to alert one another of related resources. Typically, a blog may display quotations from another blog through the use of TrackBacks.

**UDP/IP**

UDP/IP is a protocol for computer networks. It is the faster of the two primary Internet Protocols. UDP stands for **U**ser **D**atagram **P**rotocol.

**Unicode**

The Unicode character set is a superset of the ASCII character set with provisions made for handling international symbols and characters from other languages. Unicode is sixteen bit, so takes up roughly twice the space as simple ASCII, but is correspondingly more flexible.

**UNIX**

UNIX is a family of OSes, each being made by a different company or organization but all offering a very similar look and feel. It can not quite be considered non-proprietary, however, as the differences between different vendor's versions can be significant (it is still generally possible to switch from one vendor's UNIX to another without too much effort; today the differences between different UNIXes are similar to the differences between the different MS-Windows; historically there were two different UNIX camps, Berkeley / BSD and AT&T / System V, but the assorted vendors have worked together to minimalize the differences). The free variant Linux is one of the closest things to a current, non-proprietary OS; its development is controlled by a non-profit organization and its distribution is provided by several companies. UNIX is powerful; it is fully multitasking and can do pretty much anything that any OS can do (look to the Hurd if you need a more powerful OS). With power comes complexity, however, and

UNIX tends not to be overly friendly to beginners (although those who think UNIX is difficult or cryptic apparently have not used CP/M). Window managers are available for UNIX (running under X-Windows) and once properly configured common operations will be almost as simple on a UNIX machine as on a Mac. Out of all the OSes in current use, UNIX has the greatest range of hardware support. It will run on machines built around many different processors. Lightweight versions of UNIX have been made to run on PDAs, and in the other direction, full featured versions make full advantage of all the resources on large, multi-processor machines. Some different UNIX versions include Solaris, Linux, IRIX, AIX, SunOS, FreeBSD, Digital UNIX, HP-UX, NetBSD, OpenBSD, etc.

**upload**

To upload a file is to copy it from your computer to a remote computer. The opposite is download.

**UPS**

An **u**ninterrupted **p**ower **s**upply uses heavy duty batteries to help smooth out its input power source.

**URI**

A **U**niform **R**esource **I**dentifier is basically just a unique address for almost any type of resource. It is similar to but more general than a URL; in fact, it may also be a URN.

**URL**

A **U**niform **R**esource **L**ocator is basically just an address for a file that can be given to a browser. It starts with a protocol type (such as http, ftp, or gopher) and is followed by a colon, machine name, and file name in UNIX style. Optionally an octothorpe character "#" and and arguments will follow the file name; this can be used to further define position within a page and perform a few other tricks. Similar to but less general than a URI.

**URN**

A **U**niform **R**esource **N**ame is basically just a unique address for almost any type of resource unlike a URL it will probably not resolve with a browser.

**USB**

A really fast type of serial port that offers many of the best features of SCSI without the price. Faster than many types of parallel port, a single USB port is capable of chaining many devices without the need of a terminator. USB is much slower (but somewhat less expensive) than FireWire.

**uucode**

The point of uucode is to allow 8-bit binary data to be transferred through the more common 7-bit ASCII channels (most especially e-mail). The facilities for dealing with uucoded files exist for many different machine types, and the most common programs are called "uuencode" for encoding the original binary file into a 7-bit file and "uudecode" for restoring the original binary file from the encoded one. Sometimes different uuencode and uudecode programs will work in subtly different manners causing annoying compatibility problems. Bcode was invented to provide the same service as uucode but to maintain a tighter standard.

**variable width**

As applied to a font, variable width means that different characters will have different widths as appropriate. For example, an "i" will take up much less space than an "m". The opposite of variable width is fixed width. The terms "proportional width" and "proportionally spaced" mean the same thing as variable width. Some common variable width fonts include Times, Helvetica, and Bookman.

**VAX**

The VAX is a computer platform developed by Digital. Its plural is VAXen. VAXen are large expensive machines that were once quite popular in large businesses; today modern UNIX workstations have all the capability of VAXen but take up much less space. Their OS is called VMS.

**vector**

This term has two common meanings. The first is in the geometric sense: a vector defines a direction and magnitude. The second concerns the formatting of fonts and images. If a font is a vector font or an image is a vector image, it is defined as lines of relative size and direction rather than as collections of pixels (the method used in bitmapped fonts and images). This makes it easier to change the size of the font or image, but puts a bigger load on the device that has to display the font or image. The term "outline font" means the same thing as vector font.

**Veronica & Veronica2**

Although traditionally written as a proper name, Veronica is actually an acronym for "**v**ery **e**asy **r**odent-**o**riented **n**etwide **i**ndex to **c**omputerized **a**rchives", where the "rodent" refers to gopher. The acronym was obviously a little forced to go along with the pre-existing (and now largely unused) Archie, in order to have a little fun with a comic book reference. Regardless, Veronica (or these days more likely Veronica2) is essentially a search engine for gopher resources.

**VIC-20**

The Commodore VIC-20 computer sold millions of units and is generally considered to have been the first affordable home computer. It features a ROM-based BASIC and uses it as a default "OS". It is based on the 65xx family of processors. VIC (in case you are wondering) can stand for either video interface **c** or video interface **c**omputer. The VIC-20 is the precursor to the C64/128.

**virtual machine**

A virtual machine is a machine completely defined and implemented in software rather than hardware. It is often referred to as a "runtime environment"; code compiled for such a machine is typically called bytecode.

**virtual memory**

This is a scheme by which disk space is made to substitute for the more expensive RAM space. Using it will often enable a comptuer to do things it could not do without it, but it will also often result in an overall slowing down of the system. The concept of swap space is very similar.

**virtual reality**

Virtual reality (often called VR for short) is generally speaking an attempt to provide more natural, human interfaces to software. It can be as simple as a pseudo 3D interface or as elaborate as an isolated room in which the computer can control the user's senses of vision, hearing, and even smell and touch.

**virus**

A virus is a program that will seek to duplicate itself in memory and on disks, but in a subtle way that will not immediately be noticed. A computer on the same network as an infected computer or that uses an infected disk (even a floppy) or that downloads and runs an infected program can itself become infected. A virus can only spread to computers of the same platform. For example, on a network consisting of a WinTel box, a Mac, and a Linux box, if one machine acquires a virus the other two will probably still be safe. Note also that different platforms have different general levels of resistance; UNIX machines are almost immune, Win '95 / '98 / ME / XP is quite vulnerable, and most others lie somewhere in between.

**VMS**

The industrial strength OS that runs on VAXen.

**VoIP**

VoIP means "Voice over IP" and it is quite simply a way of utilizing the Internet (or even in some cases intranets) for telephone conversations. The primary motivations for doing so are cost and convenience as VoIP is significantly less expensive than typical telephone long distance packages, plus one high speed Internet connection can serve for multiple phone lines.

**VRML**

A **V**irtual **R**eality **M**odeling **L**anguage file is used to represent VR objects. It has essentially been superceded by X3D.

**W3C**

The World Wide Web Consortium (usually abbreviated W3C) is a non-profit, advisory body that makes suggestions on the future direction of the World Wide Web, HTML, CSS, and browsers.

**Waba**

An extremely lightweight subset of Java optimized for use on PDAs.

**WebDAV**

WebDAV stands for Web-based Distributed Authoring and Versioning, and is designed to provide a way of editing Web-based resources in place. It serves as a more modern (and often more secure) replacement for FTP in many cases.

**WebTV**

A WebTV box hooks up to an ordinary television set and displays web pages. It will not display them as well as a dedicated computer.

**window manager**

A window manager is a program that acts as a graphical go-between for a user and an OS. It provides a GUI for the OS. Some OSes incorporate the window manager into their own internal code, but many do not for reasons of efficiency. Some OSes partially make the division. Some common true window managers include CDE (Common Desktop Environment), GNOME, KDE, Aqua, OpenWindows, Motif, FVWM, Sugar, and Enlightenment. Some common hybrid window managers with OS extensions include Windows ME, Windows 98, Windows 95, Windows 3.1, OS/2 and GEOS.

**Windows '95**

Windows '95 is currently the second most popular variant of MS-Windows. It was designed to be the replacement Windows 3.1 but has not yet done so completely partly because of suspected security problems but even more because it is not as lightweight and will not work on all the machines that Windows 3.1 will. It is more capable than Windows 3.1 though and now has excellent driver support and more games available for it than any other platform. It is made to run on top of MS-DOS and will not do much of anything if MS-DOS is not on the system. It is thus not strictly an OS per se, but nor is it a true window manager either; rather the combination of MS-DOS and Windows '95 result in a full OS with GUI. It is partially multitasking but has a much greater chance of crashing than Windows NT does (or probably even Mac OS) if faced with a buggy program. Windows '95 runs only on x86 based machines. Currently Windows '95 has several Y2K issues, some of which have patches that can be downloaded for free, and some of which do not yet have fixes at all.

**Windows '98**

Windows '98 is quite possibly the second most popular form of MS-Windows, in spite of the fact that its official release is currently a point of legal debate with at least nineteen states, the federal government, and a handful of foreign countries as it has a few questionable features that might restrict the novice computer user and/or unfairly compete with other computer companies. It also has some specific issues with the version of Java that comes prepackaged with it that has never been adequately fixed, and it still has several Y2K issues, most of which have patches that can be downloaded for free (in fact, Microsoft guarantees that it will work properly through 2000 with the proper patches), but some of which do not yet have fixes at all (it won't work properly through 2001 at this point). In any case, it was designed to replace Windows '95.

**Windows 2000**

Windows 2000 was the intended replacement for Windows NT and in that capacity received relatively lukewarm support. Being based on Windows NT, it inherits some of its driver support problems. Originally it was also supposed to replace Windows '98, but Windows ME was made to do that instead, and the merger between Windows NT and Windows '98 was postponed until Windows XP.

**Windows 3.1**

Windows 3.1 remains a surprisingly popular variant of MS-Windows. It is lighter weight than either Windows '95 or Windows NT (but not lighter weight than GEOS) but less capable than the other two. It is made to run on top of MS-DOS and will not do much of anything if MS-DOS is not on the system. It is thus not strictly an OS per se, but nor is it a true window manager, either; rather the combination of MS-DOS and Windows 3.1 result in a full OS with GUI. Its driver support is good, but its game selection is limited. Windows 3.1 runs only on x86 based machines. It has some severe Y2K issues that may or may not be fixed.

## Windows CE

Windows CE is the lightweight variant of MS-Windows. It offers the general look and feel of Windows '95 but is targetted primarily for hand-held devices, PDAs, NCs, and embedded devices. It does not have all the features of either Windows '95 or Windows NT and is very different from Windows 3.1. In particular, it will not run any software made for any of the other versions of MS-Windows. Special versions of each program must be made. Furthermore, there are actually a few slightly different variants of Windows CE, and no variant is guaranteed to be able to run software made specifically for another one. Driver support is also fairly poor for all types, and few games are made for it. Windows CE will run on a few different processor types, including the x86 and several different processors dedicated to PDAs, embedded systems, and hand-held devices.

## Windows ME

Windows ME is yet another flavor of MS-Windows (specifically the planned replacement for Windows '98). Windows ME currently runs only on the x86 processor.

## Windows NT

Windows NT is the industrial-strength variant of MS-Windows. Current revisions offer the look and feel of Windows '95 and older revisions offer the look and feel of Windows 3.1. It is the most robust flavor of MS-Windows and is fully multitasking. It is also by far the most expensive flavor of MS-Windows and has far less software available for it than Windows '95 or '98. In particular, do not expect to play many games on a Windows NT machine, and expect some difficulty in obtaining good drivers. Windows NT will run on a few different processor types, including the x86, the Alpha, and the PowerPC. Plans are in place to port Windows NT to the Merced when it becomes available.

## Windows Vista

Windows Vista is the newest flavor of MS-Windows (specifically the planned replacement for Windows XP). Windows Vista (originally known as Longhorn) currently only runs on x86 processors.

## Windows XP

Windows XP is yet another flavor of MS-Windows (specifically the planned replacement for both Windows ME and Windows 2000). Windows XP currently only runs on the x86 processors. Windows XP is currently the most popular form of MS-Windows.

## WinTel

An x86 based system running some flavor of MS-Windows.

## workstation

Depending upon whom you ask, a workstation is either an industrial strength desktop computer or its own category above the desktops. Workstations typically have some flavor of UNIX for their OS, but there has been a recent trend to call high-end Windows NT and Windows 2000 machines workstations, too.

## WYSIWYG

What you see is what you get; an adjective applied to a program that attempts to exactly represent printed output on the screen. Related to WYSIWYM but quite different.

## WYSIWYM

What you see is what you mean; an adjective applied to a program that does not attempt to exactly represent printed output on the screen, but rather defines how things are used and so will adapt to different paper sizes, etc. Related to WYSIWYG but quite different.

## X-Face
X-Faces are small monochrome images embedded in headers for both provides a e-mail and news messages. Better mail and news applications will display them (sometimes automatically, sometimes only per request).

## X-Windows
X-Windows provides a GUI for most UNIX systems, but can also be found as an add-on library for other computers. Numerous window managers run on top of it. It is often just called "X".

## X3D
Extensible **3D** Graphics data is an XML file that is used to hold three-dimensional graphical data. It is the successor to VRML.

## x86
The x86 series of processors includes the Pentium, Pentium Pro, Pentium II, Pentium III, Celeron, and Athlon as well as the 786, 686, 586, 486, 386, 286, 8086, 8088, etc. It is an exceptionally popular design (by far the most popular CISC series) in spite of the fact that even its fastest model is significantly slower than the assorted RISC processors. Many different OSes run on machines built around x86 processors, including MS-DOS, Windows 3.1, Windows '95, Windows '98, Windows ME, Windows NT, Windows 2000, Windows CE, Windows XP, GEOS, Linux, Solaris, OpenBSD, NetBSD, FreeBSD, Mac OS X, OS/2, BeOS, CP/M, etc. A couple different companies produce x86 processors, but the bulk of them are produced by Intel. It is expected that this processor will eventually be completely replaced by the Merced, but the Merced development schedule is somewhat behind. Also, it should be noted that the Pentium III processor has stirred some controversy by including a "fingerprint" that will enable individual computer usage of web pages etc. to be accurately tracked.

## XBL
An XML Binding Language document is used to associate executable content with an XML tag. It is itself an XML file, and is used most frequently (although not exclusively) in conjunction with XUL.

## XHTML
The Extensible **H**ypertext **M**ark-up **L**anguage is essentially a cleaner, stricter version of HTML. It is a proper subset of XML.

## XML
The Extensible **M**ark-up **L**anguage is a subset of SGML and a superset of XHTML. It is used for numerous things including (among many others) RSS and RDF.

## XML-RPC
XML-RPC provides a fairly lightweight means by which one computer can execute a program on a co-operating machine across a network like the Internet. It is based on XML and is used for everything from fetching stock quotes to checking weather forcasts.

## XO
The energy-efficient, kid-friendly laptop produced by the OLPC project. It runs Sugar for its window manager and Linux for its OS. It sports numerous built-in features like wireless networking, a video camera & microphone, a few USB ports, and audio in/out jacks. It comes with several educational applications (which it refers to as "Activities"), most of which are written in Python.

## XSL
The Extensible Stylesheet Language is like CSS for XML. It provides a means of describing how an XML resource should be displayed.

## XSLT
**XSL T**ransformations are used to transform one type of XML into another. It is a component of XSL that can be (and often is) used independently.

## XUL
An XML User-Interface Language document is used to define a user interface for an application

using XML to specify the individual controls as well as the overall layout.

**Y2K**

The general class of problems resulting from the wrapping of computers' internal date timers is given this label in honor of the most obvious occurrence -- when the year changes from 1999 to 2000 (abbreviated in some programs as 99 to 00 indicating a backwards time movement). Contrary to popular belief, these problems will not all manifest themselves on the first day of 2000, but will in fact happen over a range of dates extending out beyond 2075. A computer that does not have problems prior to the beginning of 2001 is considered "Y2K compliant", and a computer that does not have problems within the next ten years or so is considered for all practical purposes to be "Y2K clean". Whether or not a given computer is "clean" depends upon both its OS and its applications (and in some unfortunate cases, its hardware). The quick rundown on common home / small business machines (roughly from best to worst) is that:

All Mac OS systems are okay until at least the year 2040. By that time a patch should be available.

All BeOS systems are okay until the year 2040 (2038?). By that time a patch should be available.

Most UNIX versions are either okay or currently have free fixes available (and typically would not have major problems until 2038 or later in any case).

NewtonOS has a problem with the year 2010, but has a free fix available.

Newer AmigaOS systems are okay; older ones have a problem with the year 2000 but have a free fix available. They also have a year 2077 problem that does not yet have a free fix.

Some OS/2 systems have a year 2000 problem, but free fixes are available.

All CP/M versions have a year 2000 problem, but free fixes are available.

PC-DOS has a year 2000 problem, but a free fix is available.

DR-DOS has a year 2000 problem, but a free fix is available.

Different versions of GEOS have different problems ranging from minor year 2000 problems (with fixes in the works) to larger year 2080 problems (that do not have fixes yet). The only problem that may not have a fix in time is the year 2000 problem on the Apple ][ version of GEOS; not only was that version discontinued, unlike the other GEOS versions it no longer has a parent company to take care of it.

All MS-Windows versions (except possibly Windows 2000 and Windows ME) have multiple problems with the year 2000 and/or 2001, most of which have free fixes but some of which still lack free fixes as of this writing. Even new machines off the shelf that are labelled "Y2K Compliant" usually are not unless additional software is purchased and installed. Basically WinNT and WinCE can be properly patched, Windows '98 can be patched to work properly through 2000 (possibly not 2001), Windows '95 can be at least partially patched for 2000 (but not 2001) but is not being guaranteed by Microsoft, and Windows 3.1 cannot be fully patched.

MS-DOS has problems with at least the year 2000 (and probably more). None of its problems have been addressed as of this writing. Possible fixes are to change over to either PC-DOS or DR-DOS.

Results vary wildly for common applications, so it is better to be safe than sorry and check out the ones that you use. It should also be noted that some of the biggest expected Y2K problems will be at the two ends of the computer spectrum with older legacy mainframes (such as power some large banks) and some of the various tiny embedded computers (such as power most burgler alarms and many assorted appliances). Finally, it should also be mentioned that some older WinTel boxes and Amigas may have Y2K problems in their hardware requiring a card addition or replacement.

**Z-Machine**

A virtual machine optimized for running interactive fiction, interactive tutorials, and other interactive things of a primarily textual nature. Z-Machines have been ported to almost every platform in use today. Z-machine bytecode is usually called Z-code. The Glulx virtual machine is of the same idea but somewhat more modern in concept.

## Z80

The Z80 series of processors is a CISC design and is not being used in too many new stand-alone computer systems, but can still be occasionally found in embedded systems. It is the most popular processor for CP/M machines.

## Zaurus

The Zaurus is a brand of PDA. It is generally in between a Palm and a Newton in capability.

## zip

There are three common zips in the computer world that are completely different from one another. One is a type of removable removable disk slightly larger (physically) and vastly larger (capacity) than a floppy. The second is a group of programs used for running interactive fiction. The third is a group of programs used for compression.

## Zoomer

The Zoomer is a type of PDA. Zoomers all use GEOS for their OS and are / were produced by numerous different companies and are thus found under numerous different names. The "classic" Zoomers are known as the Z-7000, the Z-PDA, and the GRiDpad and were made by Casio, Tandy, and AST respectively. Newer Zoomers include HP's OmniGo models, Hyundai's Gulliver (which may not have actually been released to the general public), and Nokia's Communicator line of PDA / cell phone hybrids.

CPSIA information can be obtained
at www.ICGtesting.com
Printed in the USA
BVHW011434250620
582308BV00012B/844